iPHONE® FOR SENIORS
QuickSteps®

About the Author

Marty Matthews "played" with some of the first mainframe computers, the ones that took up half a football field and still used vacuum tubes, and from those to the latest iPad and iPhone, he has never lost his fascination with computers. He has been everything from a programmer to a software company president and many steps in between. Throughout he has worked to bring others along with him and help them make the best use of all that computers can do. Toward that end, he has written over 80 books on software and computing subjects, with many becoming bestsellers and receiving a number of accolades.

His recent books include *iPad for Seniors QuickSteps®*, *Windows 8.1 for Seniors QuickSteps®*, and *Windows 8 QuickSteps®*.

Marty and his wife Carole, also a writer, are the co-creators of the *QuickSteps®* books and live on an island northwest of Seattle, Washington.

About the Technical Editor

Anne Dotson's passions are technology and education. She was an early PC adopter and is constantly exploring new software. She is a Google Certified Teacher, a Google Apps Certified Trainer, and a Microsoft Innovative Educator. Long before most people were aware of computers, Anne took computer science courses, and a very early course on the Internet and HTML put on by NASA. Most of Anne's professional career has been as a teacher, from elementary education, to home economics, to high school English and special programs. She pioneered two separate high school programs: one in character education, where she wrote three books on the subject, and the other in critical thinking, where she established a new program to teach and test the subject. Most recently, Anne has married her two passions by working as the Technology Integration Specialist in her local school district, where she introduced the iPod and iPad into the school program and brought the district teachers and staff up to speed on the subject. She is never very far from her iPad and iPhone, and when she is on the move, which is most of the time, her iPad is under her arm and her iPhone is in her hand.

iPHONE® FOR SENIORS
QuickSteps®

Marty Matthews

WITHDRAWN

New York   Chicago   San Francisco   Athens
London   Madrid   Mexico City   Milan
New Delhi   Singapore   Sydney   Toronto

Cataloging-in-Publication Data is on file with the
Library of Congress

iPhone® for Seniors QuickSteps®

1234567890   QVS QVS   1098765

ISBN   978-0-07-184399-7
MHID   0-07-184399-X

Sponsoring Editor / Roger Stewart
Editorial Supervisor / Janet Walden
Project Editor / Howie Severson, Fortuitous Publishing
Acquisitions Coordinator / Amanda Russell
Technical Editor / Anne Dotson
Copy Editor / Bart Reed
Proofreader / Lisa McCoy
Indexer / Karin Arrigoni
Production Supervisor / George Anderson
Composition / Cenveo Publishing Services
Illustration / Erin Johnson
Art Director, Cover / Jeff Weeks
Cover Designer / Pattie Lee
Series Creators / Marty and Carole Matthews
Series Design / Mary McKeon

Carole and Michael, my mainstays

Contents at a Glance

Contents

1

2

3

4   Chapter 4   **Using Email and Messages**..55

5   Chapter 5   **Managing Time and Events**..73

Acknowledgments

The author of a book is just the beginning of what it takes to produce one. The team for this book is especially accomplished and added greatly to making the book all that it is. I am most appreciative for all that they did. I particularly want to acknowledge the following people:

Anne Dotson, technical editor, who corrected many errors, added many notes and points, and did so with much enthusiasm and many kind and supportive words. Thanks, Anne!

Janet Walden, editorial supervisor, who often rolled up her sleeves and did much of the editorial heavy lifting throughout the project. Thanks, Janet!

Howie Severson, project manager, who made sure that all the pieces came together to produce the book. Thanks, Howie!

Bart Reed, copyeditor, who is so very good at making my words readable without changing my voice. Thanks, Bart!

Karin Arrigoni, indexer, who adds so much to the usability of book. Thanks, Karin!

Lisa McCoy, proofreader, who made sure that the words and illustrations actually work to tell a story that makes sense. Thanks, Lisa!

Amanda Russell, editorial coordinator, Wonder Woman, and Queen of Apple permissions who kept us on schedule with all the chapters and illustrations accounted for, an almost herculean task. Thanks, Amanda!

Roger Stewart, editorial director, who is responsible for making this book a reality for us. He has worked with us for over 25 years and never lost faith, although I'm sure he questioned it more than once. In the process, he has become a valued friend. Thanks, Roger!

I am also fortunate to live in a very supportive community that includes our local telephone, Internet, and broadband supplier **Whidbey Telecom** and its co-president **George Henny**, who provided assistance in a number of ways, not the least of which was to cheer me on. Thanks, George!

Introduction

The iPhone is the ultimate computing device for seniors. It is small, light, very portable, and very capable, allowing seniors to have with them at all times the means for making and receiving phone calls, doing email, messaging, scheduling, getting news and information, working with photos and videos, socializing, reading, listening to music, and watching movies. I believe that every senior should have an iPhone, and it is my objective to make that assimilation as easy as possible with the end result being the fullest possible use of the iPhone.

Most of my friends and acquaintances are seniors, as I am, and I have spent a fair amount of time helping them get comfortable with computers in general and the iPhone in particular. This book is written for them in a voice without jargon using relevant examples in clear, step-by-step instructions. This book zeroes in on only the most important topics, and it uses brief instructions in plain language, with many color visuals to clearly lead the reader through the steps necessary to perform a task.

QuickSteps® books are recipe books for computer users. They answer the question "How do I…" by providing a quick set of steps to accomplish the most common tasks with, in this case, an iPhone and iOS 8.

QuickSteps® are the central focus of the book, showing you how to quickly perform tasks. QuickFacts sidebars provide information that, although outside the primary discussion, is important to understand for the overall use of the iPhone. Notes, Tips, and Cautions augment the steps with concepts and thoughts that the reader needs to be aware of. The introductions are minimal, and other narrative is kept brief. Numerous full-color illustrations and figures, some with callouts, support the steps.

You can easily find the tasks you want to perform through

- The table of contents, which lists the functional areas (chapters) and tasks in the order they are presented

- A QuickSteps® To list of tasks on the opening page of each chapter

- The index, which provides an alphabetical list of the terms that are used to describe the functions and tasks

- Color-coded tabs for each chapter or functional area, with an index to the tabs in the Contents at a Glance (just before the table of contents)

Conventions Used in This Book

iPhone for Seniors QuickSteps® uses several conventions designed to make the book easier for you to follow:

- A ⬤ in the table of contents references a QuickFacts sidebar in a chapter.

- **Bold type** is used for words on the screen that you are to do something with, such as "…tap **Settings**, and tap **Calendar**."

- *Italic* type is used for a word or phrase that is being defined or otherwise deserves special emphasis.

- SMALL CAPITAL LETTERS are used for keys on the keyboard, such as ENTER and SHIFT.

- When there are several commands in a row with the same verb (for example, tap **Settings**, tap **General**, tap **Siri**, tap **On/Off**), the instruction becomes long and hard to follow. To simplify that, I have replaced the comma and repeated verb with the | character (called the vertical line or pipe character). Thus, the example becomes tap **Settings | General | Siri | On/Off**.

Chapter 1

Getting Acquainted with Your iPhone

Welcome to your iPhone! It is one of the foremost communication and information devices ever created. It allows you to communicate through voice, video, and text, as well as seek information in the form of text, sound, images, and video. You can make and receive any of the three forms of communication, as well as create, access, and exchange information on the Internet—through email, notes, or documents you write; through photos or video you take; and through appointment calendars, maps, and games you use. Your iPhone even provides a built-in voice-activated assistant to help you use it and its information. In addition to what you see on the screen when you first start your iPhone, there are over 1.2 million "apps" (applications) you can download from the App Store and run on your device.

The iPhone 6, shown in Figure 1-1 in the next section, is first and foremost a phone with which you can call any other phone in the world that's on a public exchange. It is also a fully capable handheld computer, not much different from a desktop or laptop computer except in size and shape. Although there are some limitations due to its size, such as a smaller screen and less memory, this is more than made up for by its cameras, its global positioning system (GPS), its ability to use cellular as well as a Wi-Fi Internet connection, and its considerable portability.

NOTE This book is written with the iPhone 6 or 6 Plus and iOS 8. There are many similarities with iPhone 5s, 5c, 5, and 4s and iOS 7, so this book can easily be used with earlier devices. However, I strongly recommend upgrading to iOS 8.

In this chapter you'll explore the external features of the iPhone, see how to plug it in, charge its battery, turn it on and off, put it to sleep, and wake it up. You'll then go through the iPhone setup to get an Apple ID and activate your iPhone and set up its basic services.

TIP Sign up for the AppleCare+ two-year extended warranty in the first 30 days and get two instances of accidental damage coverage, plus two years of telephone support, versus no accidental damage coverage and 90 days phone support in the free basic one-year warranty. The extended warranty currently costs $99 plus tax.

EXPLORE YOUR IPHONE

Take a moment to explore the physical iPhone and what you got when you purchased it.

▷▷ Look at the Physical Features of the iPhone

Your iPhone has several controls, sockets, and features that allow it to perform its functions. These are located on the front, back, and sides of the device. Figure 1-1 shows the front, back, and left side of an iPhone 6, which contains these components:

- **FaceTime camera** This camera has 1.2MP (megapixels, or million pixels) resolution, provides face detection, and takes 720p (progressive-scan) high-definition (HD) video.

It is used with FaceTime, the video-conferencing app that comes with the iPhone, but can also be used with other apps. See Chapter 6 for how to use FaceTime.

- **Phone earpiece** Used to hear a phone conversation.

- **On/off–sleep/wake button** The primary power controller for the iPhone. Pushing it quickly puts the iPhone in power-saving sleep mode. Pushing it quickly again or pushing the Home button wakes the iPhone from sleep. Pushing and holding this button for about three seconds begins the process of shutting the power fully off. Pushing and holding this button for a little over a second when the iPhone is powered off begins the process of powering up the iPhone.

- **iSight camera** This camera has 8MP resolution with autofocus, optical image stabilization (iPhone 6 Plus only), a five-element lens, face detection, exposure control, backside illumination, and panorama mode. It can be used for either still pictures or videos with video stabilization, continuous autofocus, 3× zoom, and 1080p HD. See Chapter 6 for more information on using the camera.

- **True Tone flash** Provides a bright light for the camera when the light sensor between the camera and the flash says it is needed. The flash can also be used as a flashlight that is turned on from the Control Center.

- **Ring/silent switch** Turns off the ringer so that the phone only vibrates if it rings. You can use Settings | Sounds to set the ringtone used and to set when the phone vibrates.

- **Volume up/down buttons** Used to change the loudness of the phone ringer and in both the speaker and whatever is plugged into the headphone jack. Press the top button to increase the volume and press the bottom button to reduce it.

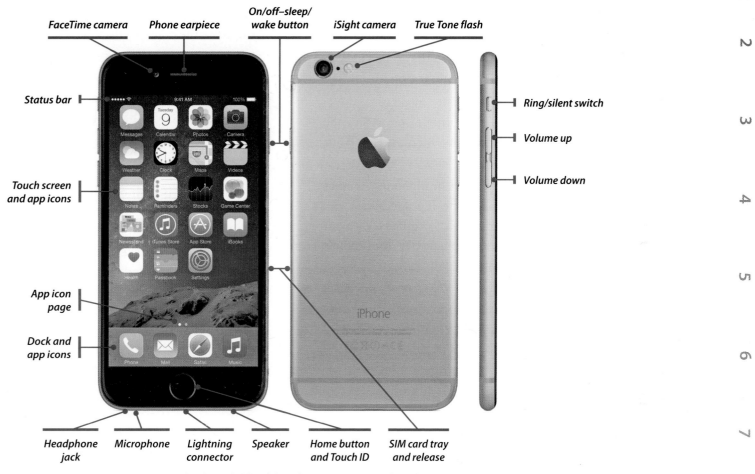

FaceTime camera   Phone earpiece   On/off–sleep/wake button   iSight camera   True Tone flash

Status bar

Touch screen and app icons

App icon page

Dock and app icons

Ring/silent switch

Volume up

Volume down

Headphone jack   Microphone   Lightning connector   Speaker   Home button and Touch ID   SIM card tray and release

*Figure 1-1: **Front, back, and side of the iPhone 6 (courtesy of Apple Inc.)***

- **SIM card tray and release hole**   You can poke a paperclip into the release hole to open the tray. The tray holds the SIM card, which identifies your phone, your network, and type of service. It normally comes already installed.

- **Home button and Touch ID**   Used to display your Home screen when pressed. From the Home screen you can open

or reopen any app on the phone and access the settings that control how the iPhone behaves. In the iPhone 6 and 6 Plus, as well as the iPhone 5S, the Home button incorporates a fingerprint identity sensor that you can use to identify yourself in place of entering a passcode.

- **Speaker** Lets you hear Siri, music that is being played, and other sounds that are produced by your iPhone.

- **Lightning connector** Used to plug in the iPhone to both charge the battery and directly communicate with another computer.

- **Microphone** Used to talk on the phone and to Siri (the voice assistant), and used with Voice Memos, FaceTime, and other apps.

- **Headphone jack** Used to plug in headphones, such as Apple's EarPods, to talk on the phone, listen to music, and hear any other audio, including Siri, produced by your iPhone. When a listening device is plugged in, the iPhone's speaker and mic are turned off.

- **Dock** Located at the bottom of the screen, the dock provides a separate area to park your most heavily used apps so you can more easily reach them independent of what other apps are displayed. You can move apps on and off the dock, but it is limited to four apps.

- **App icons** Represent the applications available on the iPhone. You start out with apps that come standard with the iPhone and in a standard layout. You can add icons and rearrange their layout on the screen, but you cannot delete the standard apps. (However, you can hide the standard apps by enabling Restrictions in Settings | General and turning off the apps you want hidden.)

- **App icon page** The dots shows which of the several app icon pages is being displayed. Two dots with the first one brighter than the other one means that there are two app icon pages and the first one is being displayed.

- **Touch screen** Also called a "multitouch screen" or just "the screen," the touch screen comprises the majority of the front face of the iPhone. It allows you to view, select, and manipulate the contents displayed there.

- **Status bar** Located at the top of the iPhone screen, the status bar provides information about the connectivity with both Wi-Fi and your cellular carrier, the current time of day, and the degree to which your battery is charged (described in Chapter 2).

Use of iPhone Memory

Inside your iPhone is memory that is used to store pictures, movies, videos, TV shows, music, books and magazines, mail, contacts, documents, and apps. Apps can also temporarily use some memory when they execute. No two people will have the same mix of these items, and there is no easy way to determine what your mix will be. Also, no one item takes the same amount of storage in every device. You have at least 16GB (gigabytes, or billion bytes) of memory and maybe more, depending on the model you have. Here are some rough rules of thumb for the amount of memory used by various items:

- Full-length commercial movies and TV shows are 1GB to 3GB.

- Videos, depending on their length and their format, take from 500MB (.5GB) to 1.5GB.

- Music takes about 1MB per minute, or about 50MB for a CD.

- Magazines depend on length and the number of photographs, but generally range from 150MB to 500MB.

- Pictures, depending on their size and quality, take from 50KB to 3MB.

- Apps vary greatly, from 50KB to over 1GB for some games.

- Documents, mail, and contacts take relatively little space.

NOTE A kilobyte (KB) is 1,000 bytes, 1,000KB is a megabyte (MB), and 1,000MB is a gigabyte (GB). A byte is roughly a character.

As you store information on your iPhone, consider your mix of movies, TV shows, music, and games. If you are around a computer where you can store these items, it is very easy to transfer items back and forth from your iPhone. You can also use iCloud for this purpose. Both of these processes are discussed later in this book.

TIP Store the bulk of your movies, videos, pictures, and music on your computer or on iCloud and only keep on your iPhone what you know you will be using in the near term.

Understand Wi-Fi vs. Cellular

Your iPhone has both cellular and Wi-Fi service capability, which allow the iPhone to connect to the Internet to communicate with the hundreds of millions of people, businesses, organizations, and institutions connected to it. This communication capability is foundational to the use of both the iPhone and its operation. The iPhone could not do what it does without this capability, which is therefore critical to its success.

If you don't already have Wi-Fi service in your home and/or office, it is easy to get from your local telephone company, TV cable company, or an independent Internet service provider. Also, it is available for free in many public locations such as libraries, coffee shops, hotels, and airports. Depending on your cellular contract, Wi-Fi might be able to save you money.

PLUG IN AND START THE IPHONE

When you first get your iPhone, the temptation is to immediately turn it on and start using it. The iPhones are shipped from the factory with enough charge in their battery to do this, but unless you had your iPhone set up at the store where you bought it, you must go through the activation and setup process. To make sure you have enough power to do all you want when you first turn it on, I recommend that you start by plugging in and charging your iPhone; it should not take more than a couple of hours. After that, you can turn it on and begin the activation and setup process.

▷▷ Plug In and Charge Your iPhone

Plugging in your iPhone is not exactly rocket science, but there are two ways to do it:

- The simplest and surest way to plug in and charge your iPhone is by using the USB-to-AC adapter, plugging it into a wall socket, and plugging the Apple Lightning-to-USB cable into both the AC adapter and your iPhone.

- You can also use the Apple-to-USB cable to connect your iPhone to a computer through a USB socket on the computer. This allows you to both charge your iPhone and to transfer information between your computer and your iPhone, as discussed later in this chapter and in several other places in this book. To charge your phone, your computer may need to be turned on.

When you have successfully charged your iPhone and have turned it on, you will see an icon in the upper-right corner of the iPhone screen that looks like a green battery with a lightning bolt to its right.

▷▷ Turn On and Set Up Your iPhone

When your iPhone battery is reasonably charged, turn the iPhone on and begin the activation process by activating your cellular service, and then go through the setup and activation process of the iPhone itself with Apple.

Activate Your Cellular Service

In the United States, four cellular companies offer iPhone service, and there are slight differences among the services concerning what you have to do to activate your cellular service. Your phone should come with instructions on how to do this, but the easiest and least troublesome way is to call customer service or go into an Apple store or a store for your cellular company and have them walk you through the process.

> **CAUTION!** If you are replacing an old phone with your iPhone 6, be sure to back up your old phone to your computer before you activate your new phone. This requires that you have iTunes on your computer, or that you use a service provided by your cellular company. Often, you can take your old and new phones into a store for your cellular company and they will back up and transfer the data from your old phone to your new one. You will need to turn off your old phone before you activate the new one.

Activate Your iPhone

When you are ready, use these steps to start and activate your iPhone:

1. Hold your iPhone in portrait fashion, where it is taller than it is wide, with the Home button at the bottom, as shown in Figure 1-1. This will orientate the iPhone for the following steps.

2. Press the **Home** button at the bottom of the phone. The screen should come on and display the word "Hello" in a number of languages.

   If the screen does not come on, press and hold the **On/Off–Sleep/Wake** button on the right side of the iPhone for several seconds. The screen should display the Apple logo for several seconds as the iPhone starts up ("boots up"). Finally, you should see the initial screen with the word "Hello."

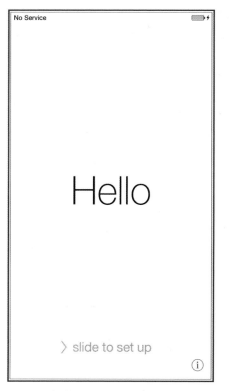

3. At the bottom of the screen, use your finger to slide the words **Slide To Set Up** to the right.

4. If you are asked to choose your language, touch (or *tap*) the language you want to use and your country (for example, "English" and "United States").

5. If there are several Wi-Fi networks around you, you will see them listed. Tap the network you want to use. If you don't see a network, none is available where you are. Tap **Use Cellular Connection** and skip to step 7. If you think you have Wi-Fi, contact your Internet provider or ask the business or organization you think is providing the Wi-Fi.

6. If you are connecting to a Wi-Fi network, you are asked to enter the password for that network. Use the onscreen keyboard that pops up to do this (see the "Using the Onscreen Keyboard" QuickFacts later in this chapter) and tap **Join**.

7. When a check mark appears next to the network you want, tap **Next**.

8. Determine whether you want to enable Location Services. This uses the iPhone's GPS and/or your cellular network to determine your current location, and is valuable when you are asking Siri about the location of restaurants or using maps. It is especially valuable when you are getting driving directions. Also, Location Services must be enabled to use Find My iPhone. On the other hand, apps can see where you are and use that information, which you may or may not want. (Keep in mind that you can turn off Location Services for specific apps in Settings | Privacy | Location Services.) I think that the benefits of Location Services outweigh the perceived loss of privacy. Based on your decision, tap either

Enable Location Services or **Disable Location Services** and then tap **Next**.

```
•••• Verizon 🛜         2:03 PM        🔋⚡
‹ Back

            Location Services

Enable Location Services                    ›

Disable Location Services                   ›


                    ↗

            What is Location Services?
Location Services allows apps like Maps and
services like Spotlight Suggestions to gather
and use data indicating your approximate
                 location.

            About Location Services
```

Set Up Your iPhone

With your iPhone started and connected to the Internet, you next need to connect to Apple to set up an Apple ID and register your iPhone. Apple uses a common ID and password for Apple itself, the iTunes Store, the App Store, iCloud, the iBook Store, and the Mac App Store. This allows you to get accounts to download apps from Apple's App Store, or music and videos from the iTunes Store, and accessories from the Apple Store. You'll need to have and use an Apple ID even for free apps and other free items. Apple doesn't charge for the ID itself, and there is no other way to work with Apple. Continue with these steps to set up your iPhone:

1. If you have used an iPhone in the past, you probably have a backup you can use to quickly set up a new iPhone. In that case, your first question is, do you want to set up as a new iPhone

or do you want to restore from an iCloud or iTunes backup? If you don't have a backup, you won't see this question. We'll assume you want to set up as a new iPhone (we'll talk about restoring in Chapter 10). Tap **Set Up As New iPhone** unless you have the choice of restoring and want to do that.

```
•••• Verizon 🛜         2:03 PM        🔋⚡
‹ Back

              Set Up iPhone

Set Up as New iPhone                        ›

Restore from iCloud Backup                  ›

Restore from iTunes Backup                  ›


                    ↺

            What does restoring do?
Your personal data and purchased content
will appear on your device, automatically.
```

2. You are then asked to either sign in with an Apple ID or create a new one. Again, we'll assume you need to create a new one (if you have an Apple ID, enter it and your password and skip to step 11). Tap **Create A Free Apple ID**.

3. Select your birthday by using your finger to move the three calendar elements up or down. When you are done, tap **Next**.

4. Tap in the **First Name** field and tap or type your first name using the keyboard at the bottom of the screen. See "Using the Onscreen Keyboard" QuickFacts later in this chapter to understand how to do that.

5. Tap **Return** to go to the next line. Type your last name and then tap **Next**.

6. If you have an existing email address, accept that default, tap **Next**, enter your address, tap **Next** again, and skip to step 8. If you do not have an email address that you want to use, tap **Get A Free iCloud Email Address**, tap **Next**, and follow on to step 7.

7. Type the first part of your new email address (for example, type **funnyclown** for an email address of funnyclown@ icloud.com). Tap **Next**. You are asked if you are sure you want to use that email address. If so, tap **Create**.

8. Enter and verify a password that's at least eight characters long and contains a number and both uppercase and lowercase letters. Tap **Next** when you are done.

9. Choose three security questions, enter their answers, and tap **Next**. If you wish, and if you have one, enter another email address that can be used in case all else doesn't work. In any case, tap **Next**.

> **CAUTION!** Write down your password and the answers to your questions so there is no way you would not know them. Make and keep a password list for yourself and give someone you trust a copy. If you are locked out of your iPhone, *no one*, not even Apple, can get you in without losing all the information on your phone.

10. If you want email updates from Apple, leave the default ON and tap **Next**. If you do not want these updates, *swipe* (move your finger across) the **ON** button from right to left to turn it off. Tap **Next**.

11. You are asked if you agree to Apple's terms and conditions. You can read them on your iPhone or have them sent to you by email. If you don't agree, you will not be able to use your iPhone. However, if it is shortly after you purchased

it (within 30 days), Apple will allow you to return the iPhone with a full refund. When you are ready and do agree, tap **Agree** and then tap **Agree** again.

12. Next you are asked if you want to use iCloud, which is Apple's free Internet storage service for backing up the information on your iPhone. If something happens to your iPhone, you can recover your information from iCloud. Also, if you store your iPhone information on iCloud, you can access that information on your iPad, iPod touch, or Mac. I think it is a good idea, and the first 5GB are free. If you want this, tap **Use iCloud**; if not, tap its alternative, and then, in either case, tap **Next**.

13. You are told that Find My iPhone is automatically enabled with iCloud, although you can turn it off later in Settings | iCloud, which is discussed later in this book. Find My iPhone is invaluable if you lose your phone or if it is stolen. Find My iPhone is good insurance, and I recommend that you keep this. Tap **Next**.

14. Next you are asked if you want to upgrade to iCloud Drive, which is similar to GoogleDrive and Microsoft's OneDrive. Tap **Not Now**. We'll come back to this topic later in the book. Tap **Continue** to confirm that you do not want to upgrade to iCloud Drive.

15. If you have used an iPhone before, you will be asked if you want to let people contact you via iMessage and FaceTime, and your phone number and email address will be displayed and selected (with a check mark). If you don't want to use either of those contacts, tap them to deselect them. In any case, tap **Next**.

16. Next you are asked if you want to use your fingerprint in place of your passcode. If you don't want to do that, tap **Set**

Up Touch ID Later and skip to step 17. Otherwise, place your finger or thumb on the **Home** button. Repeatedly lift and replace your finger on the button. When you are asked, lift, move your finger a bit, and replace it to capture the edges of your finger. Finally, you are told that the process has been completed. Tap **Continue**.

17. You are then asked to create a passcode. Even with Touch ID, a passcode is occasionally necessary for verification. Without Touch ID, a passcode is used whenever you start or wake up your iPhone to protect it from unauthorized use, and I recommend that you set one up. The standard passcode is four numbers, like the PIN you might have elsewhere. Enter your passcode and then re-enter it for confirmation.

18. Next you are asked to set up an iCloud Keychain that is used to store your passwords and credit card information with encryption. You can choose to do this or set it up later. I recommend that you go ahead and do this. Tap **Set Up iCloud Keychain**. Choose to use your existing passcode, or create a different one. You can change this later, so for now tap **Use Passcode**.

19. Enter either your phone number or the phone number of someone you trust and tap **Next**.

20. Tap **Use Siri** and tap **Next**. Siri is a voice-activated assistant to which you can ask questions, such as "What are the Greek restaurants in Bellevue?" or "Do I have an appointment next Tuesday?" You can also tell Siri to call someone or get directions. I can't imagine someone not wanting to use Siri.

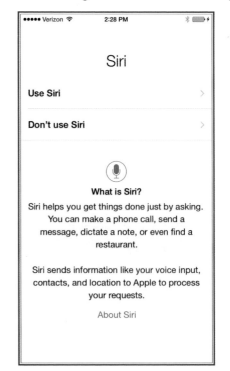

21. You can choose to help Apple by anonymously sending them information about how you are using your iPhone, including your location. I believe that doing this helps all users, so I recommend it. If you agree, tap **Automatically Send**; if not, tap **Don't Send**. In either case, tap **Next**.

22. Similarly, you are asked if you want to help app developers by having Apple share crash information and data about how you use apps with them. Again, I think this is worthwhile and recommend that you do it. If you agree, tap **Share With App Developers**; if not, tap **Don't Share**.

23. If you want larger images and text on the screen, tap **Zoomed**; otherwise, tap **Standard**. You are shown the image you have chosen. If you want to change it, tap the opposite at the top of the screen. When you are ready, tap **Next**.

24. Finally, you see "Welcome to iPhone." Tap **Get Started**. The familiar iPhone Home page is displayed.

QuickFacts

Using the Onscreen Keyboard

When you need to enter text on your iPhone, an onscreen keyboard is automatically displayed. Simply tap the keys you want to use. Here is how to use the other features of the onscreen keyboard:

- If you don't see a keyboard when a form or text entry box is displayed, simply tap in the text box in which you want to place text.

(Continued)

- To make a letter uppercase, press the upward-pointing arrow or the **SHIFT** key so the arrow itself darkens, and then tap the letter. Uppercase will automatically be turned off after you tap the letter.

- To make a series of letters uppercase, *double-tap* (tap twice in rapid succession) the **SHIFT** key so a line appears beneath the arrow. Then tap the keys you want in uppercase. When you are done, tap the upward-pointing arrow again to turn it off.

- To correct an error, tap the **BACKSPACE** key once for each letter you want to replace. Then tap the replacement key(s).

- To complete one line of type and go to the next line, tap the **RETURN** key. You may also tap the new line on the screen.

- To enter numbers and some of the special characters, tap the **123** key. If you don't see the special characters you want, tap the **#+=** key for additional characters. When you are done entering numbers and/or special characters, tap the **ABC** key to return to the original keyboard.

- With the **!** and **?** keys, press and hold the key for a moment to see two options and then press the desired key to get the character you want. There are also a number of additional choices by tapping and holding any of these keys: **- / $ & " .** and **'**.

- When you finish entering text or complete a form, the onscreen keyboard automatically disappears.

▷▷ Attach Your iPhone to a Computer

If you have a recent (in the last five years) computer available to you, either a Mac or a PC, you can attach your iPhone to it and transfer information between the two devices. To do that, you need to install Apple's iTunes on that computer if you haven't already. This is a particularly good approach if you have a lot of music or videos on the computer that you want on the iPhone. See the "Reviewing What You Need" QuickFacts earlier in this chapter for the specifications of the computer you need to use.

If you have iTunes already on the computer, make sure it is up to date. On a Mac, press the **Apple** key and click **Software Update**. On a PC with Windows 7 or earlier, click **Start**, click **All Programs**, and click **Apple Software Update**. On a Windows 8 PC, on the Start screen, start typing **Apple** and click **Apple Software Update**. You will be told if iTunes is not up to date. If so, follow the instructions to update it.

Download and Install iTunes

If you do not already have iTunes, you can download it for free from Apple and install it on your computer.

> **TIP** You do not have to use a credit card to set up an iTunes account. Simply select **None** or skip the entry when you are asked for a payment type. You, of course, will not be able to buy anything that's not free (there are many free items on both the App Store and iTunes Store). Also, you can get a very limited credit card and use that for your Apple ID and other purchases on the Internet.

1. On your computer, open a browser, type **itunes.com** in the address box and press **ENTER**. The Apple iTunes download page will open.

2. Click **Download iTunes**. On the next page, click **Download Now** (you don't have to enter your email address, and I'd uncheck the two email offers) and click **Run** at the bottom of the screen in Windows 7 and earlier versions or click **itunes64Setup.exe** at the bottom of the window in Windows 8.

3. In the Welcome To iTunes dialog box that opens, click **Next**. Uncheck any of the options you don't want, and then click **Install** and click **Yes** to allow iTunes to make changes to your computer.

4. Finally, when you are told that iTunes has been installed, click **Finish**. iTunes will open on your desktop.

Connect Your iPhone to iTunes

Once you have iTunes installed and your iPhone set up, it is time to connect the two. Here are the steps to follow:

1. Plug the Apple Lightning connector into your iPhone and the USB connector into your computer. The iPhone's screen will come on. Touch the Touch ID or swipe the **Slide To Unlock** arrow left to right and enter your passcode, if you have enabled either of these, and then tap **Trust** in the Trust This Computer? dialog box that opens.

2. If it isn't already running on your computer, start iTunes. You should see your iPhone appear in the left column. If you don't have a left column (or *sidebar*), click the **View** menu and click **Show Sidebar**. If you don't see a menu bar across the top, click the **Select** menu (the black and white rectangle) in the far upper-left corner, and then click **Show Menu Bar**.

3. Click *your* **iPhone** in the left column to open a pane on the right about your iPhone, as you see in Figure 1-2.

4. If you had a previous iPhone that you backed up, you can restore it now by selecting that option and jumping to step 6. Alternatively, you can set up as a new iPhone (if you didn't previously have an iPhone or back it up, that is the automatic selection). Click **Continue**.

5. You are told you can sync the music on your computer through iTunes to your iPhone. Click **Get Started**.

6. If, when you set up your iPhone as described earlier in the chapter, you selected to automatically back up on iCloud, it will be selected in iTunes, as you see in Figure 1-3.

7. You may additionally, or in lieu of iCloud, back up on the computer you are connected to. If so, click that option, if desired, click **Encrypt Local Backup**, enter and verify a password, and click **Back Up Now**.

You will see a lot more about syncing music, videos, and other media between iTunes and your iPhone in later chapters of this book.

 NOTE Although you can back up your iPhone to a computer, I recommend additionally, or in lieu of the computer, backing up to iCloud. The computer can be destroyed by fire or be stolen; the iCloud cannot be. If you choose to back up both to your computer and to iCloud, I recommend that you leave iCloud selected for automatic backup and manually back up to your computer.

▷▷ Turn Your iPhone On or Off and Put It to Sleep or Wake It

In going through the setup of your iPhone, you have probably experienced the screen shutting itself off automatically after the iPhone had been inactive for a period of time. This is the iPhone's sleep mode, a low-power condition that prolongs

Figure 1-2: iTunes not only allows you to transfer information, but also to control some aspects of your iPhone.

the battery life, but makes it immediately available to perform some task for you. This is one of three power modes:

- Fully powered on with the screen lit and the iPhone is available at a single touch.

- In sleep mode with the screen dark, but the iPhone is available by waking it.

- Fully powered off and not using any power. It must be turned on to be used.

Turn the iPhone On or Off

When the iPhone is fully powered off, you must start it up. You know it is off if you press the **Home** key and nothing happens (given that your battery has a charge).

- To turn off your iPhone, press and hold the **On/Off–Sleep/ Wake** button until the Power Off command appears, and then swipe that command from left to right.

Figure 1-3: iTunes allows you to perform several operations on your iPhone remotely.

- To turn on your iPhone, press and hold the **On/Off–Sleep/ Wake** button until the Apple icon appears. Then, when the **Slide To Unlock** command appears, swipe it from left to right. Enter your passcode. Even if you are using Touch ID, you must enter a passcode when starting up.

Put Your iPhone to Sleep or Wake It

By providing the sleep mode, Apple has made your battery last a lot longer. Remember that when you get tired of your iPhone

often being asleep. You can adjust the period of time before your iPhone goes to sleep, as you will see in Chapter 2.

You can wake your iPhone in two ways:

- Press the **Home** button and either swipe the **Slide To Unlock** command from left to right, and enter your passcode, or touch the **Home** button to use Touch ID.

- Press the **On/Off–Sleep/Wake** button and either swipe the **Slide To Unlock** command from left to right and enter your passcode, or touch your **Home** button to use Touch ID.

To put your iPhone to sleep, momentarily press the **On/Off–Sleep/Wake** button. (Normally, your iPhone will go to sleep automatically, but if you want, you can put it to sleep manually.)

Get Accessories for Your iPhone

A large number of accessories are available for your iPhone from both Apple (apple.com/us/iPhone/iphone-accessories) and retailers such as Amazon (go to amazon.com and search for "iPhone accessories"). Some of the accessories you can consider include cases and covers, screen protectors, cables, and headphones.

Chapter 2

Using Your iPhone

In this chapter you'll explore how the iPhone is used, beginning with its screen, how to use it and manipulate the apps on it, what those apps do, and how to, in general, use them. We'll talk some more about typing on the screen and then how to use Siri, the voice assistant, and dictation to get around having to type. Finally, we'll go in depth on using the most important app, Phone, and its related app, Contacts, to make and receive calls, manage calls, handle special situations, and keep track of and use contacts.

EXPLORE THE IPHONE SCREEN

The screen is the central focus of the iPhone. The screen is used to both control the iPhone and display an initial set of apps that the iPhone has available. Besides the few buttons along the edges or at the bottom front, the iPhone is controlled on the screen. You do it with your fingers, often with just a touch, but there are other moves of your fingers that you need to know. This section describes how to start, pause, and leave apps as well as how to navigate among them.

▷▷ Let Your Fingers Do the Work

The principal control device for your iPhone is your fingers. You don't have to remember to bring them along or learn how to use them, unlike a mouse, and their use is intuitive and simple.

Use One or Two Fingers

The principal commands used in this book can be performed with one or two fingers:

- **Tap**   Lightly touch and withdraw your hand once from an object on the screen to select it.

  - Tap an app on the Home screen to open or start the app.

  - Tap an item in a list, such as an option in a menu or a photo in an album, to select or display it.

  - Tap an action in an app, such as a previous or next arrow, to follow that action (for example, to return to the previous page in Safari).

  - Tap a text box, as in the address bar in Safari or text line in Notes, to identify the line into which the text you type will go.

  - Tap a key on the onscreen keyboard to place its character on a selected text box or text line.

  - Tap the status bar at the top of the screen when a web page, an email message, or a list is displayed to quickly move to the top of the page, message, or list.

NOTE   It is not always easy to see and tap on the status bar, which may be above the search bar.

- **Double-tap**   Tap a display on the screen twice, such as a page in Safari or a map in Maps, to generally enlarge the content being displayed.

- **Flick or Swipe**   Quickly move one finger up or down, left or right, to perform the following actions:

  - Scroll or move a web page, an email message, or a list up or down or left or right

  - Turn the pages in a newspaper, magazine, or book

  - Open the Notification Center by flicking down from the top of the screen

  - Open the Control Center by swiping up from the bottom of the screen

- **Drag**   Press and hold a finger on an object until it is selected, or, in the case of the apps on the Home screen, until all apps wiggle and then drag the object to where you want to move it.

- **Pinch**   Bring together two fingers, often your thumb and forefinger, to zoom *out* and display more area in a web page, email message, reading page, or a map, showing more area but at a smaller text size.

- **Spread**   Spread apart two fingers to zoom *in*, enlarge, and display less area in a web page, email message, reading page, or a map, but with a larger text size.

- **Press**   Press the Home button when in an app to leave the app and return to the Home screen.

- **Double-press**   Double-press the Home button to open the App Switcher, showing the apps you have used that are still active. Tap any of the apps to switch to that app. At the top of the App Switcher are your favorite and recent contacts. Tap any one of them to place a call to that person.

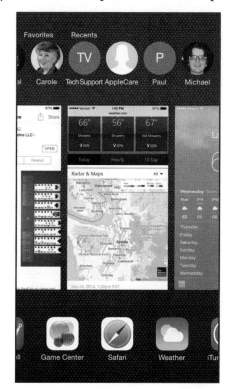

NOTE In the App Switcher, you can switch from one app to another with a single finger swipe from the right or left.

Review the Initial Home Screen Apps

On a new iPhone there are 23 apps on the Home screen, plus another seven on a second screen. The icons and their order can be different, depending on when you got your iPhone, but here are the Home screen apps in the order they appear in

iOS 8 in the fall of 2014 (see the inside of the front cover for the images, or look at your iPhone):

- **Messages** Allows you to send and receive text messages with any other device able to do the same, as discussed in Chapter 4.

- **Calendar** Allows you to enter and keep track of calendar events and sync with other calendars, as discussed in Chapter 5.

- **Photos** Stores, organizes, and displays photos that you have taken, as discussed in Chapter 6.

- **Camera** Allows you to take both still and video images from either the front or rear camera, as discussed in Chapter 6.

- **Weather** Provides the current temperature and 10-day forecast for one or more cities worldwide, with hourly forecasts for the next 12 hours.

- **Clock** Displays the time of day, temperature, and weather conditions in up to 12 locations around the world.

- **Maps** Displays maps and satellite views, gives driving directions, and shows your current position, as discussed in Chapter 7.

- **Videos** Provides the means to store, organize, and play movies, TV shows, and other videos, as discussed in Chapter 6.

- **Notes** Allows you to jot down and organize thoughts you have and then save, email, print, and delete them, as discussed in Chapter 8.

- **Reminders** Allows you to create and keep track of calendar-oriented to-do lists, as discussed in Chapter 5.

- **Stocks**   Provides information from major exchanges as well as business news and allows you to track your stock portfolio.

- **Game Center**   Provides a social networking site where you can find people to play with and get recognized for your ability to play a game.

- **Newsstand**   Provides a place to get, store, organize, and read magazines and newspapers that you have subscribed to, as discussed in Chapter 7.

- **iTunes Store**   Allows you to purchase music, movies, TV shows, and university courses, as discussed in Chapter 7.

- **App Store**   Provides a place to search for, learn about, purchase, and download additional apps, as discussed further in Chapter 8 and elsewhere.

- **iBooks**   Allows you to get, read, and organize books and PDFs from the iBook store and other sources, as discussed in Chapter 7.

- **Health**   Allows to you track and store many health and fitness measurements from other health and fitness apps or values you enter, as discussed in Chapter 8.

- **Passbook**   Provides access to Apple Pay and is a place to store and use boarding passes, movie tickets, and more, as discussed further in Chapter 8.

- **Settings**   Allows you to change the settings for the iPhone itself, as well as many of the apps. Settings is discussed further in this chapter and in many other chapters.

- **Phone**   Allows you to make and receive phone calls as well as to maintain a detailed Contacts list, as well as handle voicemail, as discussed later in this chapter.

- **Mail**   Provides an email program that allows you to send, receive, reply to, and forward email messages from one or more email accounts, as discussed in Chapter 4.

- **Safari**   Provides a web browser that allows you to search and surf the Internet, as discussed in Chapter 3.

- **Music**   Provides the means to store, organize, and play music that you have collected, as discussed in Chapter 7.

- **FaceTime**   Allows you to video-chat (conference) with anyone who has an iPhone, iPad, iPod touch, or a Mac computer for free if you are using Wi-Fi, as discussed in Chapter 6.

- **Calculator**   Allows you to perform standard calculator operations in portrait orientation or scientific functions in landscape orientation.

- **Podcasts**   Allows you to search for, select, download, and listen to or watch podcasts, as well as organize and automatically update those you choose.

- **Compass**   Provides a direction, your latitude, and your longitude, as well as allows you to find level, match a slope, and stay on course by locking in a current heading.

- **Voice Memos**   Allows you to record, play back, store, and organize voice recordings using the iPhone's microphone, the EarPods' mic, or another external microphone.

- **Contacts**   Allows you to store names, addresses, email addresses, phone numbers, and notes about people and organizations, as discussed later in this chapter.

- **Tips**   Provides tips on using your iPhone.

Understand the Status Bar

Along the top of the iPhone's screen is the status bar, which can contain a number of icons that appear at various times depending on what the iPhone or its apps are doing. Many of these icons are discussed further in this and other chapters. See the inside of the back cover for images of these icons in the following order:

- **Airplane Mode** has been turned on and all cellular, Wi-Fi, and Bluetooth transmissions by the iPhone have been turned off.

- **Connected to the cellular carrier shown** and has the signal strength indicated by the number of dots—the more, the better.

- **Connected using 4G LTE** (Long Term Evolution) service.

- **Connected using 3G** (third generation) or **4G** (fourth generation) service.

- **Connected using EDGE** (Enhanced Data for GSM Evolution) service.

- **Connected using GPRS** (General Packet Radio Service) service.

- **Making a Wi-Fi phone call**.

- **Using a Wi-Fi network** to connect to the Internet. The number of quarter-circles indicates the strength of the connection.

- **Do Not Disturb** is currently turned on, silencing all notifications and alerts, including FaceTime calls, but letting alarms still sound (see Chapter 5).

- **Personal hotspot** or Wi-Fi connection using the cellular connection to allow other devices to connect to the Internet.

- **Synced with iTunes** on your Mac or PC computer.

- **Internet activity,** such as downloading or uploading documents.

- **Call forwarding** has been turned on.

- **Connected using VPN** (virtual private networking).

- **TTY in use** to send and receive text for hearing impaired.

- **Screen rotation locked** in portrait orientation.

- **Alarm set** (see Chapter 7).

- **Location Services in use** by an app to determine your current location.

- **Bluetooth is paired** with a device, if blue. If white, it is used to communicate. If gray, the paired device is off, asleep, or out of range.

- **Battery level** of a paired Bluetooth device.

- **Battery level** and charging status of your iPhone.

Navigate Within and Among Apps

The iPhone has techniques for handling all of the many different situations that can occur when you're using apps, including using your finger alone, the Home button, and the App Switcher.

> **TIP** When you start an app, especially one of the 30 basic apps, and then start another app, put the iPhone to sleep, or even turn the iPhone off, and then come back to the first app, it is still where you left it. In other words, when you leave an app by simply starting another app or by switching away from it, the original app remains "active" (the definition of *active* depends on the app). This is what is considered "multitasking," and you can see the app in the App Switcher. In almost all cases, when you come back to the app, you will return to where you were and what you were doing when you left the app.

Navigate Within an App

There are differences in the ways that various apps work; one or more of the following techniques are used to navigate within the majority of apps:

- **Drag your finger** up or down or left or right to slowly *scroll,* or move, to other areas of the app.
- **Flick or swipe your finger** up or down or left or right to quickly scroll (move) to other areas of the app.
- **Tap a link**, such as a title, an item in a list, a picture, or a highlighted phrase, to display the page associated with that link.
- **Tap a control**, such as a left- or right-pointing arrow or a Next or Prev button, to go to the previous or next page in an app, or tap a button labeled "Buy Now," "Add To Cart," or "Sign Up" to go to the page indicated.

Leave an App

When you are done using an app, you can leave it in three ways:

- Press the **Home** button to redisplay the Home screen.
- Quickly press the **Sleep/Wake – On/Off** button to turn off the screen, lock the iPhone, and put it in sleep mode.
- Press and hold the **Sleep/Wake – On/Off** button to fully power down the iPhone.

 TIP You can think of the Home button as a "return," "go back," or "escape" key or command.

Shut Down an App

Once you start an app, it stays running—whether you are looking at it or you leave it—and is hidden in the background behind other running apps, even after you shut down your iPhone. When you turn your iPhone back on and just want to see what apps are still running, double-press the Home button to display the App Switcher. While in the App Switcher you can shut down an app by simply swiping up on it. The app will disappear from the App Switcher, and if you restart the app, it will start at its home page, not the page you last looked at.

Switch to Other Apps

When you are in one app and want to switch to another, you can use one of the following techniques:

- Press the **Home** button to redisplay the Home screen and then tap the app you want to switch to.
- Press the **Home** button twice in rapid succession to open the App Switcher and then tap the app you want to switch to.

 TIP If you don't see the recently used app you want on the App Switcher, scroll the apps by dragging them with your finger from right to left.

Go Beyond the Initial Home Screen

You have already seen that there are more built-in apps than what can fit on the initial Home screen and that there is a second screen—a second Home screen if you will. You can rearrange the app icons so they appear on whatever screen you want. In any case, the iPhone has multiple screens on which you can have apps. Just above the set of apps on the dock at the bottom of the screen are two or more white or gray dots, as you saw in the previous chapter. These dots represent alternative pages you have for the Home screen. The white dot signifies the page you are on. The gray dots are the alternatives. You can navigate among these screens by swiping to the left or right.

- Drag or swipe the screen from right to left to move to screens on the right, or from left to right to move to screens on the left.

- From any of the alternate Home screens, pressing the Home button will return you to the initial Home screen.

- From any app not on the Home screen, pressing the Home button will return you to the initial Home screen.

 QuickFacts

Searching with Spotlight

Spotlight is the iPhone's general-purpose search engine. With it, you can search the information you have stored on the iPhone, such as contacts, music, and notes, and the apps you have downloaded. It will search for apps, names, authors, artists, titles, and words, as well as email messages, appointments, and websites.

Open Spotlight

Open Spotlight to perform a search.
- From any of the Home screens, swipe down beginning at or below the first row of apps (if you swipe down from the top of the screen, you will get the Notification area).
- From any app, press the Home button and then do the "midway" swipe down.

Use Search

In the Spotlight Search box at the top of the screen, begin to type what you want to search for. As you type, items matching what you typed appear in a list below.
- If it is an app you want, tap the app name to open the app.
- If it is a contact, tap the name to open Contacts.
- If it is a song, a movie, or other media, tap the item to begin playing it.

ENTER INFORMATION INTO YOUR IPHONE

You need to enter information into your iPhone to tell it where to go, as in typing an address in Safari, or what to do, such as typing a piece of music to play. You also will probably want to add text into Mail, Messages, Notes, Reminders, Contacts, and Calendar. To do this, you can use the onscreen keyboard, as briefly described in Chapter 1, or voice dictation, which the iPhone has available.

▷▷ Expand Your Use of the Onscreen Keyboard

Chapter 1 has a brief QuickFacts to get you started using the onscreen keyboard and facilitate setting up your iPhone. Here, we will look at a number of additional features used in entering text.

Benefit from Typing Shortcuts and Aids

In addition to the primary keyboard techniques shown in Chapter 1, the iPhone has a number of shortcuts and aids to help you quickly type and correct text. Many of these, which are on by default, can be turned off in Settings, as you will see in Chapter 5. The iPhone is watching what you type and automatically helps with these features:

- **Capitalization** of the first character after a period.
- **Words** above the keyboard to correct misspellings as well as suggest logical next words. Tap SPACE to accept a highlighted corrected word or tap a suggested word to insert it.
- **Periods** and a space are added at the end of a sentence when you tap SPACE twice.

- **Phrases** are keyboard shortcuts that you type such as "btw" and "syl" to get "By the way" or "See you later." You can add shortcuts from the Home screen by tapping **Settings | General | Keyboard | Shortcuts | +**. In the Phrase text box, type the expanded phrase you want (for example, **By the way**), tap RETURN, type the shortcut (for example, **btw**), and tap RETURN again. The next time you type **btw**, you will get "By the way."

- **Apostrophes** are added to many contractions, such as "don't," "won't," and "shouldn't," when you type the word without one. Press SPACE to accept the apostrophe or touch the suggestion to reject it.

NOTE In this book, the pipe (|) character is used to replace repetitions of the leading verb. For example, instead of saying "tap **Settings**, tap **General**, tap **Keyboard**…," I'll use "tap **Settings | General | Keyboard**," making it less verbose and easier to read and follow.

- **Alternative letters** add accent marks to a character, such as è, é, and ë, when your hold your finger on the letter. Vowels are the most common characters with alternatives, but *s* and *c* have alternatives, too. Some special characters, such as the dollar sign, which shows other currency symbols, also have alternatives.

Use the Landscape Keyboard

When you turn your iPhone onto landscape orientation, where it is wider than it is tall, you'll see six additional keys that can be very useful. These include an undo key, a comma, a close key that removes the keyboard, a period, and forward and back insertion-point movement keys. If you are doing a lot of text editing, it can be worthwhile turning the iPhone to landscape orientation.

Edit Text

The iPhone gives you a number of ways to assist in editing text, including using a magnifying glass to place an insertion point; selecting the text you want to change; and cutting, copying, and pasting text as needed:

- A **magnifying glass** is displayed when you hold your finger on a piece of text. You can then move your finger to exactly place the insertion point.

- **Slide to the correct letter** when you see you are pointing at a wrong letter. Don't lift your finger off the keyboard, but slide it to the letter you want. The letter isn't selected until you lift your finger.

- **Select text**. After placing the insertion point and lifting your finger, you get the options to select the current word, select all text, or, if you have recently cut or copied something, to paste it. Tap the option you want, or you can type a character to insert it at the insertion point, or use BACKSPACE.

- **Change the selection** by dragging the blue icons at the ends of the selection.

- **Cut, copy, and paste text** options are available if you have chosen Select or Select All. Like all such computer options, Cut removes the selected text and makes it available to be pasted elsewhere. Copy leaves the selected text and makes it available to be pasted elsewhere, and Paste places the text that was most recently cut or copied at a new insertion point. There may be additional options such as Replace, which suggests alternatives to a word, and Define, which provides a definition of a word.

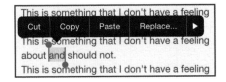

- **Shake to undo** cuts, pastes, and typing. Shake your iPhone (not too vigorously) and get a menu of undo and/or redo options pertinent to what you have just done. Tap the option you want.

▷▷ Set Up Siri and Use Dictation

Siri is the iPhone's voice assistant. It allows you to speak to the iPhone and have it respond. It can use information in your phone, as well as what it can find on the Internet. You can say, for example, "What time is my appointment with John?" and Siri will look it up in the Calendar and give you the answer. You can also say, "Where is the movie *100 Foot Journey* playing?"

and Siri will search the Internet for the answer and tell you what it found.

Turn On and Use Siri

Siri is turned on by a choice you had when you set up your iPhone. You should see a microphone key on the onscreen keyboard, as shown earlier in this chapter. You must also be connected to the Internet by either Wi-Fi or a cellular service. If you use Siri, some information about you will be sent to Apple to facilitate this use—for example, your contacts, which might allow you to say to Siri "call Home," and Siri will look at your contacts for "Home" to carry out your request. If you don't want to do that, you should not use Siri. If you don't see the microphone icon in the keyboard, you can turn it on and, in any case, begin using Siri with these steps:

1. From the Home screen, tap **Settings | General | Siri | On**.

2. To use Siri, press and hold the **Home** button until a microphone appears. When that happens, Siri will ask what it can help you with.

3. Speak in a normal voice to respond to and ask Siri any question. Siri will respond as best it can, sometimes humorously.

finished, tap **Done**. After a bit, the text you dictated will appear. It is not fast. Pause often to let it catch up. You can verbally indicate punctuation by saying the words such as "period," "comma," and "new paragraph."

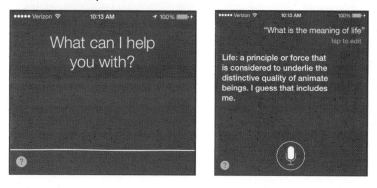

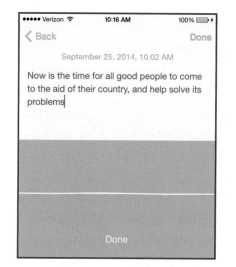

TIP As you might have seen in Settings | General | Siri, you can turn on "Hey Siri" so you can directly start talking to Siri instead of pressing and holding the Home button.

Use Dictation

The iPhone's dictation allows you to verbally add text anywhere the onscreen keyboard would normally appear. You can tell if Siri is turned on by whether a microphone key appears on your keyboard.

To use dictation, tap the microphone key (the first time tap **Enable Dictation**) and begin talking. You should see the modulated voice wave while you are talking. When you have

NOTE The reason that you must be connected to the Internet to use Siri and do dictation is that your voice is sent over the Internet to servers at Apple where it is converted to text and then sent back to you. To facilitate the conversion, Apple also collects a lot of information about you, such as your name, address, the names in your Contacts list, your current location, and so on. If you are not comfortable with this, turn off dictation by reversing the previous steps to set up Siri.

USE THE PHONE

As I said in Chapter 1, the iPhone is first and foremost a telephone with which you can easily make and receive calls using the Phone app. To facilitate that, the Phone app includes the following items:

- A numeric keypad for dialing
- A contacts list where you can store phone numbers, email addresses, and much more information
- A favorites list for frequently called numbers
- A list of recent calls both made and received
- A voicemail recorder for people to leave messages and for you to record an outgoing message

▷▷ Make Calls

Your iPhone allows you to make calls in a number of different ways, not all in the Phone app. For example, you can tap a phone number in an email or text message or on a web page to call that number. Within Phone, though, you can use the keypad, call a number in any of the three lists, and return a call from a message left in voicemail.

Make Calls from the Keypad

If you have ever made a call from a phone with a keypad, then making a call from the iPhone's keypad will be very familiar. Here are the steps to follow:

1. From the Home screen, tap **Phone**. If you don't see the keypad, tap **Keypad** on the bottom right of the screen.
2. Enter the phone number you want to call using the keypad and press **Send** (the green classic handset button).

You will hear the other phone ringing and the call screen will appear with several call options:

- **Mute**   Tap to mute all microphones either in the iPhone or in the EarPods. Touch and hold to put the call on hold.
- **Keypad**   Display the keypad to enter keystrokes during a call.
- **Speaker**   Have the iPhone behave like a speakerphone or use a Bluetooth device with the phone.
- **Add Call**   Dial another call while you are on an existing call for conference calling.
- **FaceTime**   Turn a call into a FaceTime call. (FaceTime is discussed further in Chapter 6.)
- **Contacts**   Open Contacts to get information.

When you are finished with the call, tap the red handset button at the bottom of the screen or press the **On/Off-Sleep/Wake** button, which will also put the iPhone to sleep.

Make a Call with Siri

Making a call with Siri is most intuitive: just push and hold the Home button until the microphone appears and the double-beep sounds or say "Hey Siri" and then say "Call," followed by anyone in your Contacts list or a phone number. The call will go through as if you had tapped the person in your Contacts list.

Make Calls from Lists

You can make a call from any of the three lists—Favorites, Recents, or Contacts—by scrolling the list until you see the entry and then tapping it in both Favorites and Recents. In Contacts, after scrolling to find the entry, tap it and then tap the desired phone number.

Manage the Favorites and Recents Lists

The Favorites and Recents lists can be valuable, and you'll want to maintain them and transfer entries from one list to another. The Contacts list is discussed in detail a little later in this book. The Recents list in particular needs to be culled; otherwise, it will get big fast. There are two operations that you can perform on entries in the Favorites and Recents lists:

- **Delete the entry**   Tap **Edit** in the upper right of Recents or upper left of Favorites, tap the entry, and tap **Delete** (the red circle with a white bar on the left of the entry).

- **Work with the entry**   Tap the information icon (the "i" in a circle) to open a worksheet where you can add the entry to either Favorites or Contacts (or both), make regular or FaceTime calls, send a text message, or block incoming calls.

Use Another App During a Call

If, during a call, you want to start and use another app, you can do so with iOS 8. Here's how:

1. Tap the **Home** button to open the Home screen.

2. Locate and tap the app you want to use.

3. Do whatever you want to do with the app while still talking on the phone.

4. When you are done with the app and want to return to the phone call screen, tap the green bar at the top of the screen.

▷▷ Receive Calls

When you receive a call, your iPhone will ring, vibrate, or both, and a screen will pop up with the name of the caller (if they are in your Contacts list) or the phone number (if they are not). You can then perform the following actions:

- Tap **Accept**, drag the slider if the iPhone is locked, or press the center button on your headset to talk to the caller.
- Tap **Decline**, press the **On/Off-Sleep/Wake** button quickly twice, or press and hold the center button on your headset to decline the call and send it to voicemail.
- Tap **Remind Me** to set up a reminder for the call.
- Tap **Message** to send a text message in place of the call.
- **Silence the call** by pressing the **On/Off-Sleep/Wake** button or either volume control button. The call can then be accepted or declined and sent to voicemail.

Handle Voicemail

Voicemail allows callers to leave voice messages to you on your iPhone, as well as allows you to record an outgoing message that callers hear when you can't answer your phone. Callers are sent to voicemail when you do not or cannot answer your phone as well as when you decline a call. When a caller leaves a voicemail message, you know about it in three ways:

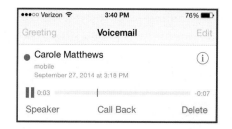

- On the lock screen, you'll see a note that you missed a call and that the caller left voicemail.

- On the Home screen, the Phone app will have a number in a red circle indicating the number of voicemail messages.

- At the bottom of the Phone app screens, you'll see a number in a red circle over the Voicemail icon indicating the number of voicemail messages.

To listen to a voicemail message, open the Phone app, tap the Voicemail icon, tap the message you want to hear, and tap **Play** (the right-pointing arrow). Tap **Speaker** to hear the voicemail there. Also, you can drag the slider opposite Play to position where in the message you want to listen. Tapping the information icon (the "i" in a circle) displays the information you have on the caller in Contacts. When you are done listening to a message, tap outside the message box to close it.

To record a greeting (the outgoing message that a caller hears when they go to voicemail), open voicemail as described previously and tap **Greeting** in the upper left. You have two choices: the default your cellular service has set up, and a custom greeting you set up on your iPhone. To create a custom greeting, tap **Custom | Record**, speak the message, and tap **Stop**. You can then tap **Play** to listen to your message, and, if desired, re-record it. When you are happy with your message, tap **Save**.

Call Waiting

Call waiting occurs when you are engaged in a phone conversation and another call comes in. If the caller is someone in your contacts list, you will see their name and possibly their picture. Otherwise, you will just see the phone number. In any case, you will get three options about what you want to do:

- **End Current Call** Hang up the original call and connect the second call.
- **Send To Voicemail** Decline the second call and keep the first call connected.
- **Hold & Accept** Put the first call on hold and connect to the second call. When you hang up the second call, you will be reconnected to the first call.

Call Forwarding

Call forwarding provides the means for you to forward calls received by your iPhone to another phone number. This can be very handy, but may not be available with all cellular services—and there may be some small differences between services that do offer it. The best solution is to call your cellular service to see how to use call forwarding. With Verizon, to activate call forwarding dial *71, the number to which you want calls

forwarded, and touch **Send** (the green circle with a handset); to end call forwarding, dial *73 and touch **Send**.

WORK WITH CONTACTS

Contacts allows you to collect phone numbers, email addresses, and other information about the people and organizations with whom you correspond or otherwise interact. Contacts is a handy address book in your iPhone.

⏩ Add New Contacts

You can add contacts directly by typing them in (see "Add Contacts Directly," later in this chapter), or you can have contacts automatically added to iPhone's Contacts in several other ways, including from the following:

- **iCloud**   Contacts are transferred from other iOS devices (iPhone, iPod, and iPad) automatically using Wi-Fi if they are synched with iCloud and you have chosen to use iCloud as described in Chapter 1. On your iPhone, tap **Settings | iCloud | Contacts | On**.

- **iTunes**   Contacts are transferred from a Windows or Mac computer if iTunes is installed on the computer and synced with the iPhone, as described in Chapter 1. In iTunes on the computer, with the iPhone connected to it, select your iPhone in the left pane and select **Info** in the top command bar. You will be told your contacts are being synced, as you see in Figure 2-1.

 NOTE   It is possible to get duplicate contacts when using both iTunes and iCloud. However, you can use both, with iTunes getting contacts from your computer and iCloud getting them from other iOS devices.

- **Facebook**   Contacts are transferred from Facebook, creating a Contacts group of your Facebook friends. On your iPhone, tap **Settings | Facebook | Contacts | On**.

- **Exchange**   Contacts are transferred from a Microsoft Exchange Global Address List. On your iPhone, tap **Settings | Mail, Contacts, Calendars | Exchange** (account) | **Contacts | On**.

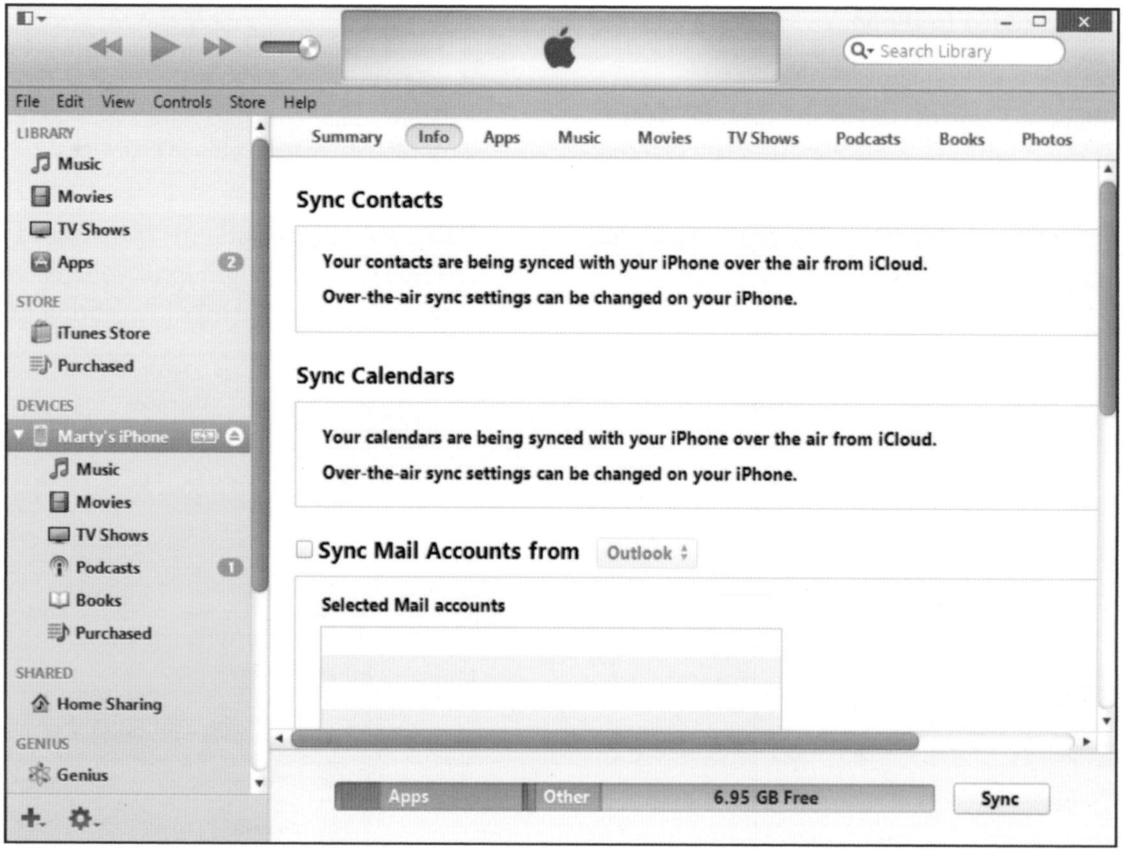

Figure 2-1: iTunes is a good conduit between email apps on your computer and iPhone, most of which are not in iCloud.

- **Mail and Safari** Contacts are picked up from incoming email or from a website, as described in the next section.

Pick Up Contacts from Mail and Web Pages

When you get a piece of email with a phone number, email address, or snail-mail address, all you need to do is touch and hold for a moment on the number or address and a menu will pop up, allowing you to add it to Contacts, among other options.

Similarly, when you are browsing through websites and find an email address, phone number, or mailing address, touch and hold on it for a moment to get a pop-up menu you can use to add it to Contacts.

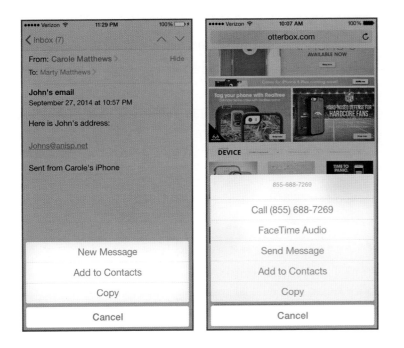

Add Contacts Directly

You can, of course, directly add individuals to Contacts, one at a time:

1. Open **Contacts** and tap the **Add** icon (the plus sign) at the top right of the All Contacts screen. The New Contact page opens.

2. Enter as much of the information as you have or want. To call, you need a name and a phone number; for email, you need at least an email address and a name. If you have additional information, such as another phone number and/or email address, or a home address for the contact, tap the text boxes for those items and fill in the desired information.

3. When you are done, tap **Done** in the upper-right corner to close the New Contact page.

TIP When you have several phone numbers or email addresses in a single contact's record, they are all displayed when you go to call the person or enter the contact in an email message so you can select the one you want.

Use Contacts

Contacts is an electronic address book you can easily carry with you and reference often. It is very intuitive and easy to use.

Call a Contact

To call a contact:

1. On the Home screen, tap **Phone | Contacts** (you can also just tap **Contacts** on the Home screen). The All Contacts list will pop up.

2. Tap the letter of the alphabet that begins the contact's last name and then tap the contact you want to call. To get more information about the contact, drag the contact's page up.

3. Tap the phone number you want to use. The call will start, and the normal calling screen will appear.

Change Contacts

To change contacts:

1. Open Contacts, locate the contact you want to change, as described in the previous section, and tap **Edit** in the upper-right corner of the contact page. A page similar to the one for a new contact will open that's filled in with the contact's existing information.

2. Make changes to any of the fields or add information to fields not already used.

3. When you are done with editing and linking, tap **Done** in the upper-right area.

Delete Contacts

To delete an entire contact entry, edit the contact to open it in editing mode, as just discussed, and then scroll to the bottom of the page and tap **Delete Contact**.

Set a Ringtone

For your special contacts (wife, husband, mother, daughter, and so on), you can set a special ringtone and/or vibration so when that person calls, you immediately know who the call is from. Follow these steps to set a ringtone:

1. Open Contacts and select the person whose ringtone you want to change.

2. In the individual's contact page, tap **Edit | Ringtone** to open a screen of alternative ringtones.

3. Touch each of the ringtones to listen to them and choose the one you want to use.

With similar steps you can change the vibration that is used for the contact as well as the text tone and vibration used when text messages are received from the person. You can set the default ringtone, vibration, text tone, and so on by tapping **Settings | Sounds**.

▷▷ Review Contacts Settings

To review Contacts settings, tap **Settings | Mail, Contacts, Calendars** and scroll down to **Contacts**. You have these settings available:

- **Sort Order**   Specifies the order in which the entries in your contacts list are displayed

- **Display Order**   Specifies how entries are shown in the list

- **Show In App Switcher**   Shows favorites and recent contacts along the top of the App Switcher

- **Short Name**   Specifies whether a short name is used and how it is constructed

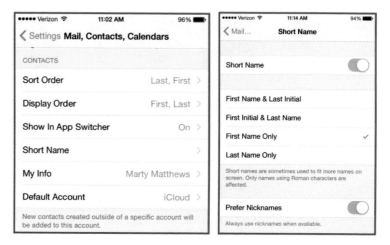

- **My Info**   Specifies the owner of or the one responsible for the list

- **Default Account**   Specifies the mail account that will be associated with contacts that aren't associated with any other mail account

Chapter 3

Exploring the Internet

The Internet provides both worldwide communication and a major means for locating and sharing information. The Internet is at the foundation of the iPhone; the iPhone wouldn't exist without it because most of what you do with the iPhone is done with the Internet. To use the Internet, you must have a connection to it using either cellular or Wi-Fi. With this connection you can send and receive email; access the World Wide Web; shop; use social networking sites such as Facebook; listen to music; watch movies and TV; and participate in blogs, forums, and newsgroups, among many other things.

In this chapter, we'll review how to get connected to the Internet, take a good look at Safari and its settings, and then see how you can use Safari to explore the Internet via both navigation and searching. Next, we'll go over how to use tabs, bookmarks, and history, and then we'll review how to get and use information on the Internet, including audio and video files. Finally, we'll cover how to control Internet security.

CONNECT TO THE INTERNET

With a cellular service, you sign up with AT&T, Sprint, T-Mobile, or Verizon (in the United States), start your iPhone, tap the Safari icon, and you are on the Internet. With Wi-Fi, you can use someone else's connection, such as in a coffee shop, library, hotel, or airport, often for free (we'll talk about how to connect there in a moment). If you want Wi-Fi in your home or office and don't already have a connection, you can get one from a local telephone company, a cable TV company, a satellite link, or an independent Internet service provider (ISP). If you already have Wi-Fi available in your home or office and just need to connect your iPhone to it, skip to "Use the World Wide Web" a little later in this chapter.

▷▷ Establish an iPhone Wi-Fi Connection

To use your iPhone in a Wi-Fi area, called a "hotspot," you must tell the iPhone about it and probably give the iPhone the password for the hotspot. When you first enter a Wi-Fi hotspot that you want to use with your iPhone, after turning on your iPhone, follow these steps:

1. Tap **Settings | Wi-Fi** and turn Wi-Fi on if it isn't already. Review the list of Wi-Fi networks that are available at your location.

2. Tap the wireless network you want to use. If there is a lock symbol for this network, indicating that a password is required, a Password dialog box will appear.

3. If needed, enter the network password and tap **Join**. You will be connected to the Wi-Fi network and, in most cases, to the Internet.

USE THE WORLD WIDE WEB

The *World Wide Web* (or just the *Web)* is the sum of all the websites in the world—examples of which are CNN (shown next), Amazon, and the BBC. The World Wide Web is what you can access with a web browser such as Safari.

▷▷ Get Familiar with Safari

Safari comes standard with the iPhone and provides an excellent means to access the Internet and do anything it is possible to do with a web browser. Several other browsers, including Google Chrome, are available as apps you can download from the App Store, but this book assumes you are using Safari to access the Internet.

Review Safari's Controls

Start Safari and review its controls (from the iPhone's Home screen, tap **Safari**). At the top and bottom of the Safari screen are a series of icons and features that let you control it. From left to right, these are as follows:

Address and search bar

Reload

Previous Next Share menu Bookmarks, Reading List, Shared Links Tabs

- The **address and search bar** allows you to type in a web address, or URL, to open the website in Safari. For example, if you wanted to open CNN, you would type **cnn.com** in the address bar. This same bar also allows you to enter keywords to use in searching the Internet, as you might do directly in Google. As you will see in the next section, you can select the search engine that is used to do the searching for this field. Google is the default, but Yahoo! and Bing are also options in Settings | Safari.

- **Reload** lets you re-download the selected web page from its server to see any changes in the page, such as late-breaking news or the latest prices on an auction site. If a web page is not behaving the way it should, reloading it can often fix the problem. While a webpage is being loaded, the Reload icon is replaced with a Stop icon (an X) that, if you click it, will stop the loading of the web page.

- **Previous and Next** let you return to the pages you have visited previous to or following the present page.

- The **Share menu** allows you to tap various actions you can take to share the current website address, including AirDrop to a nearby iPhone, iPad, or iPod; text messaging or emailing it to a friend; putting it on Twitter or Facebook;

adding it to your Home screen; printing or copying it; and adding it to either your Bookmarks or Reading List.

- **Tabs** identify separate website pages you have opened; simply tap a tab to see its page.

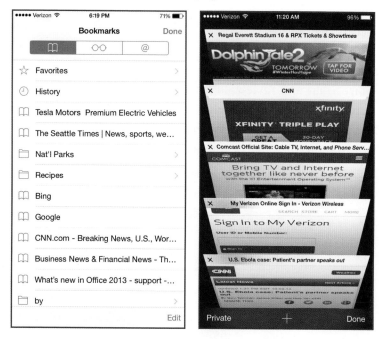

- **Bookmarks, Reading List, and Shared Links** opens a set of three lists: one for the bookmarks (website pages) that you tap to keep, one for web pages with articles you want to come back and read, and one for web pages that have been shared with you.

 TIP When you see a web address such as http://www .amazon.com, all you have to type is **amazon.com** (the "http://www." is assumed). If you have been to the site recently, you only have to type enough of the name for it to be unique; as you see in the illustration, typing **amaz** got me Amazon.com.

Look at Safari's Settings

In iPhone's Settings, there is a full set of settings for Safari. From the Home screen, tap **Settings | Safari**.

Safari's settings include the following:

- **Search Engine** allows you to choose the search engine used: Google (the default), Yahoo!, or Bing.

- **Search Engine Suggestions** allows you to turn off search engine suggestions and only display the most likely result of the search.

- **Spotlight Suggestions** allows Safari to use your Spotlight search history, including the suggestions you selected to determine the top suggestions in the current search.

- **Quick Website Search** allows you to search within a website by including the website address in the search. For example, entering **Amazon Quicksteps** displays suggestions of *QuickSteps* books on Amazon.

- **Preload Top Hit** allows Safari to immediately start loading what it determines is the most likely search result page based on your bookmarks and browsing history.

- **Passwords & AutoFill** allows you to turn on or off the automatic filling out of web forms with your contact information, including names, passwords, and other information that you have previously given to a website. This is turned off by default, and it is a good idea to leave it that way. Although it is a handy feature, it can lead to giving out information when you don't want to do so.

- **Favorites** allows you to establish the defaults that are suggested when you enter an address or search term.

- **Open Links** allows you to control whether clicking a link or opening a new page replaces the current page in the current tab or opens a new tab displaying the new page.

- **Block Pop-ups** allows you to prevent a website from opening a second little window for whatever purpose.

Here again, history has colored the prevailing view of pop-ups. They can be a pain if they are giving you information you don't want, but if they open a web form you need to fill out, they can be useful. The default is **On**, blocking pop-ups. Depending on what you are doing, you might want to turn this off.

- **Do Not Track** allows you to turn on or off the prevention (if it is on) of collecting information, such as websites you visit and your name, address, and other information you have entered into web forms. With Do Not Track on, AutoFill does not collect information and it doesn't fill in forms. Also, the history of the websites you have visited is not maintained.

- **Block Cookies** allows you to choose whether you want to accept cookies that are stored on your iPhone: either always, never, or only from sites you visit. (Cookies are small snippets of information that identify you to the website based on information you gave them.)

- **Fraudulent Website Warning** tells the iPhone to warn you when you are visiting a website that is not what it seems to be and is suspected of phishing. Phishing sites masquerade as a real site, such as your bank, and fraudulently ask you to enter your personal information, such as username and password. If you get such a warning, you want to immediately leave the site and not enter any information.

- **Clear History** and **Website Data** allow you to remove the information on your iPhone from or about the websites you have visited.

- **Use Cellular Data** tells the iPhone that it can use your cellular network to save Reading List information to iCloud for offline reading.

- **Advanced** provides three more options:
  - **Website Data** show you which websites are storing how much information on your iPhone.
  - **JavaScript** allows you to turn off accepting programs or apps that use JavaScript, a programming language. Generally, you want to leave JavaScript turned on. Many apps legitimately use it, and if you want to use the app, you have to accept the use of JavaScript. Historically, bad things were done with JavaScript, and, of course, they still can be. However, if you are running apps from the App Store, they are reasonably safe. Apple has vetted these apps.

- **Web Inspector** allows you to open Safari on your computer, connect the computer to your iPhone with a cable, and look at what a website is doing on the iPhone using Safari's Advanced Preferences option on your computer. The Web Inspector option is for use by app developers to debug (remove problems from) their apps.

⏩ Browse the Internet

Browsing the Internet refers to using a browser, such as Safari, to go from one website to another. You can browse to a site by directly entering a site address, navigating to a site from another site, or using the browser controls. First, of course, you have to open the browser.

Enter a Site Directly

To go directly to a site, follow these steps:

1. Open Safari, tap in the address bar, and tap the **X** on the right of the bar to erase the current contents.

2. Begin typing the address of the site you want to open. The iPhone will give you suggestions and fill in the address bar. I got these after typing **gopro** and needed to only tap the first suggestion to go to the site. I could also have typed **gopro.com** and tapped **Go** to open that web page.

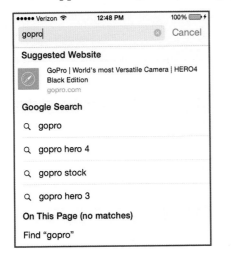

TIP The onscreen keyboards that appear when the address bar is tapped change the label of the **RETURN** key to **GO**.

Use Site Navigation

Site navigation uses a combination of links and menus on one web page to locate and open another web page, either in the same site or in another site.

- **Links** are words, phrases, sentences, or graphics that, when tapped, take you to another location. They are often a different color, banded (as "Learn More"; see the following left image), or underlined.
- **Menus** contain one or a few words in a horizontal list (as in "Standard Surf Music"; see the following right image)

or vertical list (or both) that, when tapped, take you to another location.

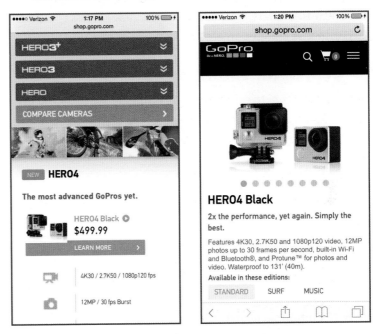

If you hold your finger on a link or a menu option, which is really a link within a menu, a pop-up menu will be displayed, allowing you to open the link in the same tab, open it in a new tab, add it to your Reading List, or copy it, allowing you to paste it in an email, text message, or elsewhere.

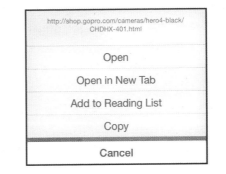

Use Browser Navigation

Browser navigation uses the controls on your browser at the top and bottom of Safari, as described in "Review Safari's Controls," earlier in this chapter, to go to another location.

Search the Internet

You can search the Internet in two ways: by using the search facility built into Safari and by using an independent search facility on the Web.

Search from Safari

Tap in the address/search box at the top of the Safari screen, tap one of the popular sites or a site you have visited, or begin to type a site name to search for sites you have recently visited or search for sites that contain keywords. For example, type **veal**. The search engine—Google is the default—will display several suggested web pages while you are typing, as well as whether there are any matches on the current web page. You can tap any of the suggestions to open those pages.

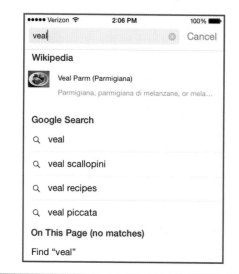

Search from an Internet Site

There are several directly accessed Internet search sites. Among these are Google, Bing, and Yahoo! Because Google is the default, you can open Google by simply tapping Go on the keyboard to display its search results. For example, with the word "veal" as entered in the previous section, you would get these results:

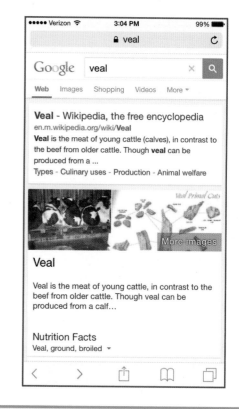

> **TIP** When you enter search criteria, place quotation marks around certain keywords or phrases to get only results that match those words exactly.

Save a Bookmark

Sometimes, you visit a site that you would like to return to quickly or often. Safari has the ability to save sites as bookmarks for easy retrieval.

Add a Bookmark

To save a site to the Bookmarks list, follow these steps:

1. Open the web page you want to add to your Bookmarks list, and make sure its correct address (URL) is in the address bar.
2. Tap the **Share menu** icon in the bottom center and then tap **Add Bookmark**. The Add Bookmark dialog box will open (see the following left image).
3. Adjust the name as needed in the text box (you may want to type a new name you will readily associate with the site).
4. Initially, the Location option is "Favorites," meaning that the link will be saved to the Favorites bar. If you tap that option, though, you can choose to save the link to the Bookmarks list or to a subfolder you have within Bookmarks (see the following right image).
5. Choose where you want to save the link and tap **Save**.

Save to the Home Screen

You can choose to have a link to a website added to the Home screen as you would an app. Here's how:

1. Open the web page you want to add to your Home screen, and make sure its correct address (URL) is in the address bar.
2. Tap the **Share menu** icon and tap **Add To Home Screen**. The Add To Home dialog box will open.
3. Adjust the name as needed in the text box and tap **Add**. You'll see the icon for the page appear on the Home screen.

Organize Bookmarks

Safari provides two places to store your bookmarks: a Bookmarks list and a Favorites list.

> **TIP** The web pages you have pinned to the Home screen from Safari can also be organized in any way you want.

Rearrange, Edit, and Delete Bookmarks

The items on your Bookmarks list are displayed in the order you added them, with the name you left them with, but you can move them to a new location, edit their names, and delete them. Follow these steps:

1. In Safari, tap the **Bookmarks Reading List Shared Links** icon and then, if needed, tap the **Bookmarks** segment on the left. Tap **Edit** on the bottom right. The Bookmarks editing features are displayed.

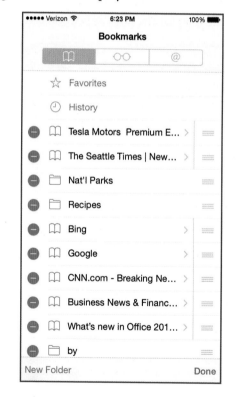

2. Locate the site you want to reposition. Touch and hold the three bars (grip strip) on the right of the bookmark, and drag it up or down to where you want it.

3. To edit a bookmark's name, tap the right arrow on the mid-right of the bookmark to open the Edit Bookmark dialog box.

4. In the top text box, edit the name as you would edit other text on the iPhone (see Chapter 2).

5. In the bottom text box opposite Location, tap the greater-than sign and tap where you want to store the bookmark (see the following section).

6. To delete a bookmark, tap the delete icon on the left of it and then tap **Delete**. When you are done editing bookmarks, tap **Done**.

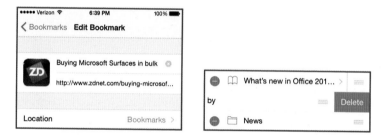

Create New Folders

You can add your own folders within Bookmarks:

1. In Safari, tap the **Bookmarks Reading List Shared Links** icon and then, if needed, tap the **Bookmarks** icon and tap **Edit** on the bottom right. The Bookmarks editing features are displayed, as you saw earlier.

2. Tap **New Folder** in the lower left, type the name for the folder, tap where you want to store the folder, and tap **DONE** on the keyboard.

3. Use the steps in the "Rearrange, Edit, and Delete Bookmarks" section earlier to move the desired bookmarks to the new folder.

Put Bookmarks in Folders

You can put a site in either your own folders (see "Create New Folders") or the default Bookmarks list and Favorites bar, which operate like folders. Here's how:

1. Open the web page you want in your Bookmarks list, and make sure its correct address, or URL, is in the address bar.

2. Tap the **Share menu** icon, tap **Add Bookmark**, adjust the name as needed in the text box, tap **Location**, tap the folder to use, and tap **Save**.

USE INTERNET INFORMATION

Of course, the reason for accessing the Internet is to use the information you find there—to read it, save it, play its media, or send it to a friend.

▷ Work with a Web Page

An iPhone screen displaying a web page in Safari works just like any other iPhone screen and gives you the same tools you've used elsewhere on the iPhone. In Safari, you can perform the following tasks:

- **Select pages**, links, items, and options by tapping them.
- **Move a page** being displayed up or down, left or right, by dragging it with your finger.

- **Change a page** by swiping from right to left or bottom to top.
- **Enlarge a page** by spreading two fingers apart.
- **Reduce a page** by pinching two fingers together.
- **Enlarge just an article** if it is in a separate frame by double-tapping the article.
- **Scroll just an article** if it is in a separate frame by dragging with two fingers.
- **See a link's destination** by touching and holding the link, which also allows you to open the link in a new tab and add it to the Reading List.

- **Fill out a form** by tapping the first field, typing what is requested, and then tapping **Next** or **Previous**.

- **Return to a web page you have viewed** by tapping the **Tab** icon in the lower right and tapping the page you want to return to. On the Tab list screen you can go to a new page by tapping the plus sign in the bottom center (see earlier illustration).

⏩ Read Web Pages

Safari has a reader with which you can separate out an article from advertisements and make reading an excellent experience.

1. Navigate in Safari to an article you want to read and then tap it. On the left end of the address bar you should see the Reader icon (a stack of lines).

2. Tap the **Reader** icon. The article will appear, filling the screen.

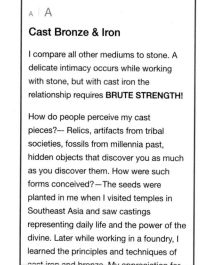

3. Scroll by swiping up (from bottom to top) as you would any other page.

4. To close the Reader, tap the **Reader** icon again in the address bar.

NOTE The Reader provides a good way to forward an article because it removes the ads and transfers just the article. Use the Share menu to do this, which works with the Reader as well.

⏩ Play Internet Audio and Video Files

You can play audio and *some* video files on the Internet with Safari directly from a link on a web page. The exception is that the iPhone cannot play video files that use the Adobe Flash technology (several apps are available in the App Store, such as the Rover browser, that will allow you to play Flash content). Many web pages have links to audio and video files, such as the one shown next. To play these files, simply tap the **play** button in the center. The player will open to play the requested piece.

> **TIP** To search for information within an open web page in Safari, type the keywords you want to search for in the Search field in the upper-right area, and then tap the entry or entries under **On This Page**.

Control Internet Security

As you read earlier in this chapter, Safari Settings allow you to control several aspects of Internet security. You can determine how you want to handle cookies placed on your computer by websites and use Do Not Track to prevent the website from bothering you in the future, among several other settings. These controls are found in Settings.

Handle Cookies

Cookies are small pieces of data that websites store on your computer so that they can remind themselves of who you are. These can save you from having to constantly enter your name and ID. Cookies can also be dangerous, however, letting people into your iPhone where they can potentially do damage. Safari lets you determine when you will block cookies:

1. In the Home screen, tap **Settings | Safari**.
2. In Safari Settings, tap **Block Cookies**.

3. Consider the four choices you have:

- **Always Block** means that every time you visit a site, you must sign in, and there is no memory of your last visit that might take you back to what you were doing the last time you were on the site.

- **Allow From Current Website Only** is a onetime exception for the current website.

- **Allow From Websites I Visit** means that you will allow cookies from the specific website you visit but block cookies from third parties and advertisers.

- **Always Allow** means that any site you come across can add whatever information they want.

The default, and my recommendation, is Allow From Websites I Visit. In my mind, cookies can be more of a benefit than a problem. You can see who has stored information on your iPhone by tapping **Advanced** at the bottom of Safari Settings and then tapping **Website Data**, as discussed earlier in this chapter.

Use Do Not Track

Safari's Do Not Track option in Safari Settings gives you a way to visit a website and not leave any information on both your iPhone and the visited website that you had visited it. This allows you to take a peek at a website and not leave any trace so as to more safely browse and view websites. While you have Do Not Track turned on, your browsing history, temporary Internet files, and cookies are not stored on your iPhone, preventing anyone looking at your phone from seeing where you have browsed. In addition, a *request* is passed on to the Internet content provider (the site you visit) *not* to track your visit. It is *up to the site* to honor that request or not!

NOTE If you are using your iPhone in a school or business that has security controls, they may be able to see where you have browsed, even with Do Not Track, and it is not perfect at preventing a website from knowing who you are.

Turn On Private Browsing

Private Browsing, which is turned on at the bottom of the Tabs screen, is another aspect of Do Not Track. If you tap **Private** on the Tabs screen, your screen will darken, Safari will not remember the sites you visit, they will not be stored on the Tabs screen, and cookies and other information will not be stored on your phone. Also, the sites will be *requested* not to track you.

Enable Fraudulent Website Warning

Fraudulent sites are websites that present themselves as legitimate ones—including banks, brokerages, email services, and others—when in fact they are not and only want to get information from you, such as your user ID, password, Social Security number, and other information. This is called *phishing*. If Fraudulent Website Warning is enabled, Safari will warn you when it thinks a site you are visiting is suspected of phishing. This is enabled by default, and I strongly recommend that you leave it that way. Safari's ability to do this is less than perfect, so you need to be aware of this practice and watch out for it.

GATHER INFORMATION AND SHOP ON THE INTERNET

The World Wide Web is a phenomenal source of information and place to shop. It is the world's largest library, museum, and shopping mall rolled into one—you only need to use it, which you can do with your iPhone and Safari.

▷▷ Search for Information

We have discussed using Safari to browse and search the Internet, but not where that takes you and what to do when you get there. There are, of course, millions of subjects you could search on, but let's look at two examples: researching a historical figure (Theodore Roosevelt) and gathering demographic information (the population growth in the 10 largest U.S. cities).

Research Theodore Roosevelt

In Safari, simply typing **theod** provides several places to start. The first, Wikipedia, is a huge online encyclopedia maintained by everybody who wants to contribute to it. The second is the

official White House presidential bio. The third is a general search on the name. Tapping the Wikipedia entry provides a wealth of information that you can read and use as needed. Tapping the general search provides numerous other sites and resources.

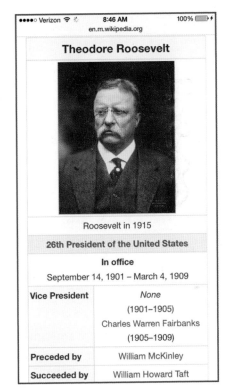

Gather Demographic Information

Here, to get what we want I had to fully type **growth of ten largest us cities**, but I got numerous sites to explore and many related searches. You have to look at several to get the information you want.

Shop on the Internet

As with sources of information, there are innumerable places to buy goods and services on the Internet; you only need to search for them. Two examples are a small black leather purse and French restaurants in Seattle.

Look for a Black Purse

My wife wanted a classic small black leather purse and hadn't seen one lately in stores, so she turned to the Internet. Typing **small black leather purse** produced a number of firms offering that product. Selecting any one or more of those sites offered many items to select from.

Find a French Restaurant

If you live in or near a large city, you know that restaurants come and go fairly quickly, so if you like a particular type of food, Internet searching can be helpful. Here is a search for French restaurants in Seattle.

Tapping on most of them opens a map and reviews, and further tapping opens a website for the restaurant with menus, photos, and reservations.

▷▷ Use Siri to Browse the Internet

Many times you can use Siri to do the searching for you. For example, you can say, "Hey Siri, get information on Theodore Roosevelt" or "find French restaurants in Seattle." Siri does an excellent job getting information on "T.R." and providing a

list of French restaurants. In the latter case, Siri goes on automatically to display the first restaurant listed and offers to make reservations for you.

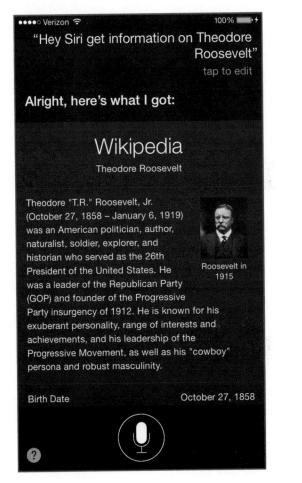

Chapter 4

Using Email and Messages

For many people, email and messaging have become primary means of communicating and are another reason for them to have an iPhone. The iPhone comes with the Mail, Messages, and Contacts apps already installed. In addition, the App Store has many alternatives for emailing and messaging. To use any apps for emailing and messaging, however, you must have a connection to the Internet and an email account. If you do not yet have an Internet connection, go back to Chapter 3 and set one up now.

This chapter will discuss getting an email account; setting up the Mail and Messages apps; sending, receiving, and managing email; and sending and receiving text messages.

USE MAIL

The iPhone's Mail app allows you to send, receive, and manage email over the Internet. This book primarily focuses on the use of the Mail app because it is a modern email program that works well and comes with and is designed for Apple's iOS. You can also send and receive email through other email apps, as well as web mail accounts using Safari, but this chapter will be devoted to using Mail.

⏩ Set Up Mail

To begin the use of Mail, you must establish an email account with an email provider recognized by Mail and then convey that information to Mail.

You may have already automatically set up Mail during your iPhone installation using the email account you used for your Apple account. If so, you can skip to "Change Mail Settings."

Establish an Email Account

For an email account, you need the following:

- An email address (for example, mike@anisp.com).
- The password for your mail account.
- You may also need to know the type of mail server you are using—either IMAP or POP (if you have a choice, choose IMAP; it is newer and provides more flexibility). Internet Message Access Protocol (IMAP) keeps a copy of your mail on the server and does not delete it until you do or until some set time, such as three months. This allows you to read your mail on several devices until you delete it on one of them. Post Office Protocol (POP) allows you to download your messages once and then deletes it on the server, unless you choose otherwise, making it hard to use it with both an iPhone and a computer.

At the time this was written, Mail recognizes accounts with iCloud, Microsoft Exchange, Gmail, Yahoo!, AOL, Microsoft Hotmail, Microsoft Outlook, and a number of smaller email services. Because you had to have an email account to get an Apple ID to use iPhone, you can generally use that for your Mail account. It is also likely that when you set up an Internet connection, you were given an email account that you can use. Finally, you can open Safari and go to Google.com, Yahoo.com, Outlook.com (not the Office product, but the replacement for Hotmail), and others to create a new account. Here are the steps with Google:

1. On the Home screen, tap **Safari**. Tap the address bar, tap the delete icon, and type the site from which you want an email account—in this case, type **google.com**.

2. Tap **More** (the three bars on the left) | **Gmail** | **Create An Account**. Enter your name, choose a username, create and confirm a password, and complete filling out the registration form.

3. When you are done, tap **Next Step**. To confirm your entries, tap **Create Profile**.

4. At the Welcome message, tap **Continue To Gmail**.

5. You are asked if you want the Gmail app. Because you already have the native iPhone Mail app, for the moment, I suggest you ignore the Gmail app and tap **Go To The Mobile Site**. This shows you your Google mail in Safari. For now, close Safari.

The Gmail account in Safari is called "web mail" and is one of three ways to look at Gmail. The other two are a Gmail app you can download and the iPhone's Mail app, which is the way we'll use. After creating an email account, put aside looking at your mail and return to the Home screen to set up Mail.

Set Up Gmail in Mail

With a Gmail account, you not only can view your mail in a web mail account on Safari, but also set it up in Mail. Here's how:

1. In the Home screen, tap **Mail**. If you have not previously set up an account in Mail, it will display a number of mail servers. Tap **Google**. If you have previously set up an account in Mail, follow the instructions in "Set Up Outlook .com in Mail," substituting "gmail.com" for "outlook.com."

2. Enter your name, email address, password, and a description of the account and then tap **Next**. If you want, choose to link Contacts, Calendars, and Notes to Gmail and then tap **Save**. Your Gmail account will open in Mail.

TIP A blue dot next to a message in your Inbox indicates that a message has not been read.

Set Up Outlook.com in Mail

Outlook.com (which used to be Hotmail, the Microsoft mail service, and may in some cases have been moved to live.com) is set up in Mail in a similar way to Gmail, but once you have any account configured in Mail, you start in a different way. If Outlook.com is your first account, start with step 1; otherwise, start with step 2.

1. In the Home screen, tap **Mail**. Mail will display a number of mail servers. Tap **Outlook.com** and skip to step 3.

2. If you have other Mail accounts, from the Home screen, tap **Settings | Mail, Contacts, Calendars | Add Account | Outlook.com.**

3. Enter your email address, password, a description of the account, and tap **Next**. Choose if you want to link Mail, Contacts, Calendars, and Reminders to Outlook and tap **Save**. You are returned to Settings.

> **TIP** Besides the major six email servers, there are a great number of other mail servers you can access on your iPhone, including smaller email servers and email on a personal website.

Change Mail Settings

Mail settings include settings for each account, as well as for Mail itself.

Change Account Settings

The account's settings vary by account and can go into a fair amount of technical depth, most of which, if you have been able to complete the setup, you don't need. The general Mail settings are discussed under "Change General Mail Settings," later in this chapter. Here's how to view the settings for a particular account:

> **TIP** If you are having trouble setting up a mail account, the quickest solution is to contact the mail provider (or Internet service provider, called the ISP) or IT help desk, either online or by phone, and have them lead you through the setup. They will help you with the detail settings for your account.

1. Tap **Settings | Mail, Contacts, Calendars |** *account name* (for example, "Gmail").

2. The account's top-level settings will open. Here, you can turn on or off portions of the mail service, delete the account, and, by tapping **Account**, go into the account's detail settings.

3. In the detail settings, you can change your basic logon information and open the advanced settings for your mail

provider. For the latter, I'd recommend that you make any changes with the help of the mail provider.

> **NOTE** Some mail providers, Gmail in particular, provide the ability to archive messages that you might want, but might not want them to take up room on your iPhone. See the discussion under "Archive, Delete, and Recover Messages," later in this chapter.

Change General Mail Settings

The general settings that apply to all mail accounts are below the account-specific settings discussed earlier. As mentioned there, tap **Settings | Mail, Contacts, Calendars** and scroll down a bit. The general settings include the following:

- **Fetch New Data** allows you to choose how you receive your email from your mail provider. You essentially have three choices, with some subchoices. From the Mail, Contacts, Calendars settings, tap **Fetch New Data**. On the screen that opens, you have these choices that affect all services:

- **Push** Your mail is automatically pushed to you by the server whenever the mail is available, causing the iPhone to be more active and, therefore, using more of the battery. Only some mail services provide the Push option (in the examples here, it is only iCloud), and you can turn that off by tapping the **On/Off** button.
- **Fetch** The iPhone's Mail app requests the server to send you your mail. This can be done automatically every

15 minutes, 30 minutes, hourly, or manually (meaning you determine when to download your mail). Manually puts the least drain on the battery. Tap the option you would like.

Individual mail services' settings can be changed by tapping the service you want to change and then tapping the selection you want from the following options:

> **NOTE** With Push email, the email is received whenever it is available, provided the iPhone is not powered off, even when it is sleeping and regardless of whether the Mail app is active. With Fetch set to a time interval (15 minutes to hourly), mail is received only when Mail is first opened and then periodically on the time interval, so long as Mail remains open. With Fetch set to manual, email is only received when you manually drag down the top of the Inbox with your finger.

- **Preview** allows you to determine the number of message lines you want displayed in the Inbox.
- **Show To/Cc Label** adds a label to received emails telling you if you are an addressee or a Cc. If no label appears, the email probably came from a mass mailing and may be spam.
- **Flag Style** allows you to select the style and color of the flags attached to mail messages.
- **Ask Before Deleting** gives you a warning and a second chance when you delete a message.
- **Load Remote Images** allows photos to be received with email when they are attached.
- **Organize By Thread** organizes your email by subject instead of time and date.
- **Always Bcc Myself** sends a copy of an email to you so you can get it on another computer, such as your desktop or

laptop computer, if you share an email account with that computer.

- **Mark Addresses** highlights addresses in your mail *not* ending in a certain domain, such as anisp.com.

- **Increase Quote Level** increases the indentation of replies and replies to replies in the list of messages in your Inbox. This works particularly well when you organize your messages by their thread (subject).

- **Signature** allows you to enter a block of text that is added at the end of your email messages. If you want to have different signatures for each of your email accounts, tap **Signature**, tap **Per Account**, and add to or replace the default "Sent from my iPhone" text with the signature block you want to use.

●●●●● Verizon 1x	4:50 PM	✻ 100% ▭ ⚡

‹ Mail...   **Signature**

All Accounts   ✓

Per Account

Cheers!
Marty Matthews

Sent from my iPhone

- **Default Account** allows you to specify the email account to use when you send email from an app other than Mail (such as Notes or Photos) and you tap the **Share** icon and tap **Mail**.

▷▷ Send, Receive, and Respond to Email

The purpose of email, of course, is to send messages to others, receive messages from them, and respond to the messages you receive. Mail does this with a simple elegance.

Create and Send Email

To create and send an email message, follow these steps:

1. Tap **Mail** on the Home screen and in the page that opens, tap the **New** icon in the upper-right corner. The New Message screen will open.

2. Start to enter a name in the To text box. If the name is in your Contacts (see "Use Contacts" in Chapter 2), it will be suggested in a list and you can tap to accept that name. If the name is not automatically completed, finish typing a full email address (such as tim@apple.com) and then tap RETURN.

●●●●○ Verizon 1x ⚡	4:58 PM	✻ 100% ▬ ⚡

Cancel   **New Message**   Send

To: rog   ⊕

Roger Stewart
roger.stewart@mheducation.com

Roger Stewart   ⓘ
other

Roger & AMANDA   ⓘ

3. If you want more than one addressee, after accepting a suggested name or tapping RETURN after typing one, as directed in step 2, you can simply begin typing a second address after the space that has been added.

●●●●○ Verizon 1x ⚡	5:01 PM	✻ 100% ▬ ⚡

Cancel   **New Message**   Send

To: Roger Stewart, ca   ⊕

Carole Matthews
home

4. If you want to differentiate the addressees to whom the message is principally being sent from those for whom it is just information, tap **Cc/Bcc** to open text boxes for those items and then enter the desired addressees there as you did in the To text box. If you want to send the message to a recipient and not have other recipients see to whom it is sent, tap the **Bcc** text box and then type the address(es) to be hidden. (Bcc stands for "blind carbon copy.")

5. Tap in the **Subject** text box and type a subject for the message.

6. Tap the area beneath the line under Subject and type your message.

7. When you have completed your message, tap **Send** in the upper-right corner of the message. If you are done, close Mail.

Receive Email

Mail can be received automatically if the account is pushing messages to the iPhone or if you have the account set on automatic fetch. Otherwise, you need to manually download your mail by dragging down the Inbox on the screen. You can tell whether you have received email on the Home page by a number in the upper-right corner of the Mail icon. Once you have unread mail in your Inbox, you can follow these steps:

1. Open **Mail** (the number opposite the mail account is the number of unviewed messages) and tap one of the accounts that contains newly received messages.

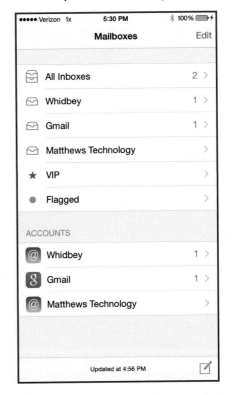

2. You can tell which messages in the Inbox are newly received by the blue dot beside them. Tap a message to have it displayed so you can read it.

> ••••• Verizon 1x   5:30 PM   ∦ 100% ⬛ ⚡
>
> ‹ Whidbey   **Inbox**   Edit
>
> Q Search
>
> ● **Marty Matthews**   5:29 PM ≫
> Schedule
> It will be implemented. -----Original
> Message----- From: Marty Matthews Sent: Tu...

3. If you wish, you can delete a message while it is selected by tapping the **Delete** icon at the bottom-center of the screen.

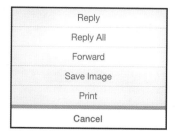

Respond to Email

You can also respond to messages you receive. Simply tap the message in the message list and then tap the **Reply** icon on the right of the screen. Alternatively, you can swipe across the message in the Inbox and tap **More | Reply**.

From the menu that appears, you can tap one of the following options:

- **Reply** To return a message to just the person who sent the original message.
- **Reply All** To return a message to all the people who were addressees (both To and Cc) in the original message.
- **Forward** To relay a message to people not shown as addressees on the original message.
- **Save Image** To save on your iPhone an attached image or an embedded image that you received in the original message. (This is only present when there is an attachment.)
- **Print** To print the original message.

> Reply
> Reply All
> Forward
> Save Image
> Print
> Cancel

In the first three cases, a window similar to the New Message window opens and allows you to add or change addressees and the subject as well as to add a new message.

▷▷ Apply Formatting

In iPhone Mail, you can add bold, italic, and underline formatting to the words, phrases, and paragraphs in an email message. You can also indent paragraphs. Follow these steps:

1. Create a new email message or one that is in response to a message you have received, as described in the previous sections of this chapter.

2. Type the text you want in the message and then tap the text you want specially formatted. The Select bar will appear; tap **Select**.

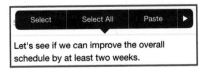

3. When the text is selected, drag the ends of the selection box as needed to select the words you want to format.

4. If it isn't already displayed, tap the selected text to open the Cut, Copy, Paste ... bar.

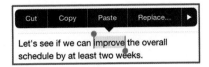

5. Tap the right-pointing arrow to display the B*I*U, Define, ... bar.

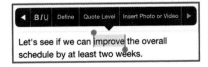

6. Tap B*I*U to open the Bold, Italics, Underline bar.

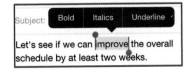

7. Tap the style(s) you want to use (you can use more than one). When you are done, tap outside of the selection.

8. To indent a paragraph, select it and open the Select bar, as done previously in step 2.

9. Tap **Quote Level**, and then tap either **Decrease** or **Increase** to outdent (move to the left) or indent (move to the right), respectively. You can do this several times if you choose. When you are done, tap outside the selection.

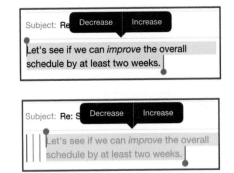

▷▷ Handle Attachments

When you send email, you may want to include a photo, a video, a note, an iWorks (Pages, Numbers, and Keynote) document, a Safari web page, or one of many other items on your iPhone. You can do that either while you are working on a message or while you are looking at the item.

TIP A number of apps have a Share icon that allows you to email the items produced by that app, among other actions. If you don't see a Share icon or other command that allows you to email an item, you can always take a screenshot of it (press and hold the **Sleep/Wake** button while pressing the **Home** button) and then email the resulting image from Photos.

Add a Photo to a Message

From within an email message, you can attach a number of documents, including photos and videos, without leaving the message. Let's look at attaching a photo as an example:

1. Create a new email message or one that is in response to a message you received, as described in the previous sections of this chapter.

2. Type the message you want to start with. When you are at the spot where you want to insert the photo, tap RETURN twice to leave a blank line.

3. Press and hold for a moment on the blank line to open the Select bar, tap the right arrow, and then tap **Insert Photo Or Video**.

4. A list of your photo folders will appear. Tap the folder, tap the photo, and then tap **Choose**. The picture will appear in your message.

Here's an alternative method:

1. When you are at the point described at the end of step 2 in the preceding list, you can also press **Home** and tap **Photos** to open the Photos app.

2. Open the album needed to locate the photo you want. Then press and hold for a moment on that photo to have the Copy, Hide bar pop up.

3. Tap **Copy**. Press the **Home** button and tap **Mail**. The email message that you have been working on will appear.

4. Press and hold for a moment on the blank line to open the Select bar and then tap **Paste**. The photo will appear in your message.

5. When you are ready, send the message as you would normally.

Email Items Directly

In the preceding section, you saw how to insert as well as cut and paste items into an open email message. You can also send photos and other items directly from their respective apps.

1. Open the app with the item you want to email. In that app, navigate to where you can see the item.

2. Select the item, tap the **Share** icon, and tap **Mail**. A new email message pops up containing the item you selected.

3. Add the addressees, a subject, and any message you want to include. When you are ready, tap **Send**.

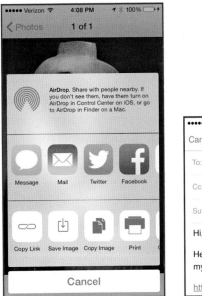

 NOTE Email that is sent directly from an app other than Mail is sent using your default mail provider, as described earlier in "Change General Mail Settings."

Handle Received Attachments

You also may need to handle attachments you receive in email on your iPhone. You can tell if a message has an attachment by the paperclip icon in the message header. The attachment can be a photo, video, or other document, including Microsoft Word, Excel, and PowerPoint files, as well as Adobe PDF files and web pages. To process an attachment, follow these steps:

1. Open a message with an attachment as you would any other message. The body of the message will open, and at the bottom you will see the attachment.

2. Tap the attachment to open it. If the attachment is a document that the iPhone can open, it will do so and you can read or view it. If you want to save it, tap the **Share** icon and then tap the app that you want to save it in. In the case of the Word document, choose **Open In Pages** or **Open In Office Mobile**, where it is automatically saved.

3. If the attachment is a photo, it will automatically open in Mail and you can save it by pressing and holding on the photo to open the Share menu. Tap **Save Image** to place it in your Camera Roll.

4. If the attachment is not a common file type, you can normally re-send it in another email, or store it in a note or cloud app. Tap the attachment to see what options are available. Here, you can see that a file created with a program called Xara (a graphics program I use with my website) can be re-sent in email or stored in Evernote, OneNote, DropBox, or OneDrive.

Manage Email

Mail allows you to organize your mail in both existing and new folders; to archive, delete, and recover messages; and to flag, mark, and search your messages.

Understand Email Folders

Email that you receive and send is stored in folders, both in the Mail app on the iPhone and the mail server you are using, as shown earlier. The folders you have available depend to some degree on the mail service and, if you have previously used it on another computer, how you set it up there. In the latter case, the iPhone will mimic the folder structure on your computer.

Here's how to work with folders:

1. From an Inbox, the most common working area of Mail, tap the mail provider's name in the upper-left corner. This may take you to the set of folders for that particular mail provider or to Mailboxes, depending on where you originally started. If you are showing Mailboxes, tap an account in the lower part of the screen to see the folders for that account.

2. If you are displaying the folders for a provider, tap **Mailboxes** in the upper-left corner. This shows you your mail accounts, both in terms of their Inboxes at the top, where tapping any of the accounts takes you to their Inbox, and the accounts themselves in the lower part of the screen, where tapping takes you to the set of folders for that account.

Add and Delete Folders

If you find that you would really like to have additional folders to better organize your mail, you can do that easily. Here's how:

1. From the Mailboxes screen, shown in the previous section, tap in the Accounts area the mail provider where you want the extra folder. The list of existing folders for that provider will appear.

2. Tap **Edit** at the top-right corner of the screen and then tap **New Mailbox** in the bottom-right corner.

 NOTE Some folders in Mail can be moved, have their name changed (which might satisfy the need for a new folder), and deleted, whereas other can't. You can tell which can be edited after you tap **Edit** because they are darker.

3. Tap an account under All Inboxes to open and observe the respective Inbox. Then return to Mailboxes by tapping the provider's name in the upper-left corner.

4. Tap an account under Accounts to open and observe the set of folders for this account. Tap **Inbox** to open and observe the Inbox arrived at in this manner. You can see there is no difference in the Inboxes.

5. Return to Mailboxes by tapping first the provider's name in the upper-left corner and then tapping **Mailboxes** in the same location.

Understanding this navigation from Mailboxes to account folders to Inboxes and back is important to easily getting around Mail.

3. Type the name for the new folder and then tap the account field beneath **Mailbox Location** to choose where in the current folder hierarchy you want the new folder.

4. Tap where you want the new folder and then tap **Save** in the upper-right corner.

5. If you want to change the position or name of the new folder, or any other folder, tap **Edit** in the upper-right area and then tap the folder you want to change.

6. In the Edit Mailbox screen, make any desired changes to the name, tap **Mailbox Location**, tap the new parent folder, and tap **Save**.

7. If you want to delete a folder, perform step 5 and then in Edit Mailbox, tap **Delete Mailbox**. Confirm that by tapping **Delete** again and then tapping **Done**.

Organize Messages with Folders

Use the various folders that you have by moving your mail among them:

1. From Mailboxes, tap an account in the upper part of the screen to open the Inbox for that account. Alternatively, tap an account in the lower part of the screen to open another folder for a given mail provider to display the message(s) you want to move to other folders.

2. Tap the message you want to move so it is displayed on the right of the screen.

3. Tap the folder icon at the top of the screen. The mail account's folders will be displayed.

4. Tap the folder in which you want to store the message. The message will disappear from its current folder and appear in its new one.

TIP There are two special mailboxes that display only messages from very important people (VIP) and those that have been flagged. You can select from your contacts those people who are VIPs.

Archive, Delete, and Recover Messages

You may have noticed that when you open a message in Gmail in the icons in the bottom area there is, by default, an archive box, whereas in other mail providers there is a trash can. This is because Gmail allows you to "archive" a message as well as to delete it. Archiving is an intermediate step between placing an item in a normal folder and deleting it.

- To delete or archive a message, open the message and tap either the delete or archive icon.

- If you choose Archive, you are given the choices of Trash Message or Archive Message.

- To recover a message, move it to a new folder using the technique described in "Organize Messages with Folders," earlier in this chapter. (Go to Mailboxes and tap the account in the lower part of the screen to display that account's folders.) Deleted messages are in either the Trash or Deleted Messages folder; archived messages are in the All Mail folder.

- Determine whether or not to use archiving, if it is available, from the Home screen. Tap **Settings | Mail, Contacts, Calendar |** *account name* **| Account | Advanced | Archive Mailbox** or **Deleted Mailbox**.

Delete, Move, and Mark Several Messages at Once

Mail has the means to delete, move, and mark a number of messages at one time:

1. Open the folder containing the messages you want to delete, move, or mark.

2. Tap **Edit** in the upper-right corner of the screen.

3. Tap the messages you want to work on. A white check mark will appear in a blue dot on the messages that are selected. (You unfortunately can't use Mark All, which only allows you to "Flag" or "Mark As Read," if some messages are unread, or "Mark As Unread" if all are read.)

4. Tap the command button at the bottom of the screen for the action you want to carry out:

   • If you tap **Trash**, the selected items go into the Trash folder for that account.

   • If you tap **Move**, the list of folders for that Mail account will open and you can tap where you want the messages to move to.

   • If you tap **Mark**, a menu pops up giving you the choice to flag the message, mark it as unread, or move it to the Junk folder, if such a folder exists.

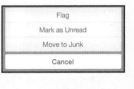

Search Messages

As the number of messages you have in various mailboxes begins to stack up, it may become difficult to find a message that you want to look at. You can use Mail's Search feature for that purpose. Search, though, searches all folders of all accounts; you can't just search a single folder.

1. Open a Mail account and folder.

2. Swipe down the list of messages. The search text box will appear at the top of the messages.

3. Type the keywords to search on. As you type, Mail will begin to select messages that match what you're typing and display their headers in the screen.

USE MESSAGES

Messages allows you to send and receive text messages using an email address or cellular phone number with any device, phone, or tablet that will receive them. It will also send and receive media messages that include photos and videos using Apple's iMessage, instant messaging (IM or *chat*) with other iPhone, iPod, iPad, and Mac (Mountain Lion and later) users who are online at the same time as you.

▶▶ Start and Use Messages

Messages, by default, is in the upper-left corner of the Home screen. The use of iMessage requires your Apple ID, which you must have to use your iPhone. As a result of that, you will automatically be signed in when you open Messages.

1. From the Home screen, tap **Messages**. Messages will open.

2. If you see a To text box, tap in it and begin to type a name. If you don't see the To box, tap the **New Message** icon in the upper-right area of the screen. If you want to search for a name, tap the **Add A Contact** icon on the far right to open the list of your contacts. Scroll down and tap the contact you want to chat with.

3. Tap the text tray at the bottom of the screen, type your message, and tap **Send**.

4. If you have a photo that you want in the message, you can attach it by tapping the **Photo** icon and tapping either **Photo Library** or **Take Photo Or Video**. In the former case, select the photo, tap **Choose**, and tap **Send**. In the latter case, select the front or back camera, tap the shutter release, and then, if you are happy with the photo or video, tap **Use Photo.**

5. If your correspondent has an iPhone or other recent Apple device, you can send voice messages using Messages. Tap and hold the microphone icon while speaking your message. A set of three controls will appear on the right, an arrowhead in the center to play back what you have recorded, an "X" to delete what you recorded, and an up arrow to send the voice message.

6. Continue the conversation as your correspondent replies. Touch the arrowhead to play an audio or video message.

▷▷ Review Messages Settings

The Messages settings, opened by tapping **Settings | Messages**, provide these options:

- **iMessage**   Allows you to turn iMessage on and off.
- **Send Read Receipts**   Provides a notice to the sender when you have read their message.

- **Send As SMS**   Uses Short Message Service (SMS), which is text only, when iMessage is not available if turned on; otherwise, Multimedia Messaging Service (MMS) is used.
- **Send & Receive**   Lets you set the addresses and phone number where you can be sent messages and from which you can send messages.
- **MMS Messaging**   Turns on Multimedia Messaging Service, which allows audio, video, and photographic images to be sent with or as text messages.
- **Group Messaging**   Allows multiple people to share a text message conversation.
- **Show Subject Field**   Allows you to display the Subject field or not.
- **Character Count**   Provides a count of the number of characters when SMS or MMS is being used, if turned on.
- **Blocked**   Opens your Contacts and allows you to select those from whom you do not want to receive messages or FaceTime calls.
- **Keep Messages**   Allows you to choose the length of time to keep text messages—from 30 days, 1 year, or Forever.
- **Audio Messages Expire**   Provides two choices: After 2 Minutes and Never.
- **Raise To Listen**   If this option is selected, raising the phone to your ear automatically starts playing an audio message.
- **Video Messages Expire**   Provides two choices: After 2 Minutes and Never.

Chapter 5

Managing Time and Events

The iPhone provides several apps or areas—including Calendar, Reminders, Clock, Notifications, and Control Center—to help you control the events of your life. This chapter provides a review of all of these, showing you how to set them up, handle their settings, and use them in several circumstances.

SET UP AND USE CALENDAR

The primary purpose of a calendar, of course, is to keep track of upcoming events, such as meetings, appointments, birthdays, and anniversaries. You can also note date-related objectives, such as projects to be completed (book deadlines, in my case) and goals to be accomplished (such as weight loss by a certain date). Whatever the purpose, Calendar has tools to work with it and several views to look at it.

▶▶ Get Familiar with Calendar

The iPhone Calendar has implemented on the screen four views of calendar entries and given you easy ways to navigate among them. Open Calendar by tapping its icon on the Home screen. One of Calendar's four views will appear.

Explore Calendar Views

When the iPhone is held upright, in portrait orientation, the four Calendar views are as follows:

- **Day view** Displays the events in one day and provides a time-of-day display on the left and the detail for events in that day on the right. The day view is similar to the day books that were popular before computers. You can swipe the dates at the top of the screen to display different days as well as swipe the screen up and down to see other times.

- **List view** Provides a summary list of events for as many days and months as there is room on the screen. You can swipe up or down to see additional events. I like to use this view as my primary one because I can keep track of a number of events.

- **Month view** Provides a high-level view of the month with the current day shown within a red dot. Each day with an event has a gray dot beneath the date. Swipe up and down to see additional months.

- **Year view** Displays 12 months on one screen with the current day marked with a red dot. Year view primarily allows you to select the month in which you want to work. Swipe up and down to see additional years.

When you hold the iPhone horizontally, in landscape orientation, all the views change to a week view with times down the left side. You can swipe the dates at the top to display other dates and swipe the screen up or down to see other times.

Review Calendar Controls

When the iPhone is in portrait orientation, the calendar has three permanent controls at the bottom as well as two to four controls at the top, which are detailed here from left to right:

- **Month or Year Selector**   Allows you to go from the current day to the current month, and from the current month to the current year. This control disappears in year view.

- **List Selector**   Opens the full events view if the screen was displaying a day, or a partial events list if the screen was displaying a month. If you are displaying the month view and want the full list of events, display a day first and then events.

- **Search**   Opens a search text box where you can enter keywords on which to search Calendar.

- **Add Event**   This is the plus icon at the top right, which opens the Add Event screen with which you enter events into the calendar.

Across the bottom from left to right are the following items:

- **Today**   Identifies the current day in the current view.

- **Calendars**   Opens a list of the various calendars you have available. From this list, you can choose which you want to display, if not all of them. Also, by tapping the "i" in a circle for one of the calendars, you can choose which color you want to represent that calendar.

- **Inbox**   Displays the calendar invitations you have received and lets you reply to them.

Change Calendar Settings

The calendar settings, opened by tapping **Settings | Mail, Contacts, Calendars** and scrolling down to the bottom of the screen, include the following:

- **Time Zone Override** Changes the default from showing events in the local time zone the iPhone is in to a selected time zone.

- **Alternate Calendars** Allows the display of Chinese, Hebrew, and Islamic dates.

- **Week Numbers** Displays the number of the week within the year in day, week, and month view.

- **Show Invitee Declines** Shows if an invitee has declined an invitation.

- **Sync** Lets you automatically sync historical as well as future events. Tapping this option allows you to select among several time periods.

- **Default Alert Times** Determines when alerts are created for birthdays, events, and all-day events. For each, you have a choice of when the alert is posted, from the time of the event to one week before the event.

- **Start Week On** Lets you specify which day of the week is on the left of a weekly calendar.

- **Default Calendar** Lets you specify which calendar to use with events that are created outside of Calendar.

▷▷ Use Calendar

The iPhone's Calendar app is made for active use as you are on the go. It will sync the entries you have from your desktop or laptop computer or such online calendar resources as Facebook and Google Calendar. It is also a good resource for directly entering and managing events as you go along.

Choose Your Calendar

Depending on your email accounts and what you have on computers and tablets, you may have a number of calendars. To start, I'd recommend that you work with only one. Later in this chapter we'll come back and look at how to handle multiple calendars.

If you have multiple calendars, begin by turning off all but one. You can then use it for the next several sections until we get to the discussion of multiple calendars.

1. From the Home screen, tap **Calendar** and then tap **Calendars** in the bottom-middle area. You will see the list of your calendars.

2. If you have other calendars turned on (they have a check mark beside them), tap all but one calendar to turn them off.

3. Tap **Done** at the top-right of the screen to close the list of calendars.

Select a Date

Calendar events, of course, are on a certain date or series of dates; therefore, the first task in using Calendar is to select a date. You have several options, depending on where you are looking:

- If you are in year view, tap the month with the event and then tap the day.
- If you are month view, tap the day.
- If you are in day or week view, drag the dates at the top of the screen to display the correct week and then tap the day if you're in day view.

Add Calendar Events

With a day selected in day view, here's how to add an event and its specifics:

1. Tap the icon for **Add Event** in the top-right corner of the screen to open the New Event screen.

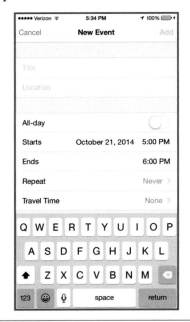

TIP You can also open the New Event screen by pressing and holding for a moment on a day and time in day or week view. A colored box will appear under your finger with the words "New Event."

2. Type the title of the event, tap in the **Location** text box, and type the location.

3. If it is an all-day event (or close enough to call it that), tap the **On/Off** button for that.

4. Tap **Starts** to open the date and time rotator. Move your finger up and down on the date to select it and then do the same thing with the hour, minutes, and AM/PM to select the start time.

5. If you want a different time zone than your current location, tap the **Time Zone** selection, if needed, and tap **Done**.

6. Tap the **Ends** time and select the appropriate time.

7. If you want a time zone other than your default, tap **Time Zone**, begin typing a different time zone, and tap the time zone that appears in the list.

8. If the event will happen periodically, tap **Repeat** and then tap the period of repetition.

9. If it is a factor, tap **Travel Time**, turn it on, and enter a starting location (if relevant), and/or select a time and tap **New Event** in the upper-left corner.

b. To add more invitees, tap the **Add** icon (the plus sign) to open your All Contacts list and then tap the person you want to invite. Repeat this for as many people as you want to invite.

c. When you are finished adding invitees, tap **Done**.

12. Tap **Alert** and then tap when you want the alert. Repeat this for the second alert if desired.

13. The default is to show your time as being "Busy" when you have an event. This is for shared calendars so others will not schedule events for you during that time. If you want to change from "Busy" to "Free," tap **Show As** and tap **Free**.

14. If desired, you may type in a uniform resource locator, or URL (that is, a web address), and enter notes for the event. When you are ready, tap **Add** to complete the event.

15. Tap the event to see its information.

10. Tap **Calendar** if you want this event listed on a calendar other than the default (see "Work with Multiple Calendars," later in this chapter), and tap **New Event** to return there, if necessary.

11. If you want to invite people to the event, tap **Invitees**.

a. Begin typing a name in your Contacts list. When the name that you want is displayed, tap that name.

For the URL and notes sections of a new event, you can copy and paste information from a website that might be of interest to the people you are inviting to an event.

Change Calendar Events

Changing an event is very easy:

1. With Calendar open on the screen, select the date of the event, as described earlier in this chapter.

2. In day, week, or month view, tap the event and tap **Edit** to open the Edit Event screen.

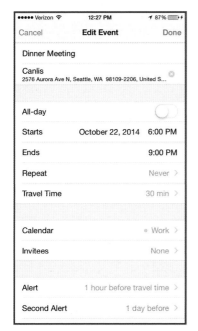

3. In the Edit Event screen, tap the field you want to change and make the desired changes. See "Add Calendar Events," earlier in this chapter, for field-by-field considerations.

4. When you have made the changes that you want, tap **Done.**

Delete Calendar Events

Deleting events is even easier:

1. Follow steps 1 and 2 in "Change Calendar Events" immediately preceding this section.

2. In the Edit Event screen, scroll to the bottom and tap **Delete Event**. Tap **Delete Event** a second time to confirm it. If the event is repeated, you will have a choice of deleting the current event only or this and all future repetitions of the event.

Work with Multiple Calendars

As you begin to use Calendar, you may find that you are getting events from several sources that you would like to keep on different calendars so you can manage them as a group. Also, you probably want to look at all your calendar events together periodically on one calendar display. The iPhone provides ways to do both of those.

When you start up your iPhone for the first time after setting it up and syncing to iCloud, you will see that, by default, Calendar with iCloud starts out with three independent calendars, labeled "Home," "Work," and "Birthdays." You can, therefore, immediately place events on more than one calendar.

Add Events to a Different Calendar

To add events to one of several calendars, you can use one of three techniques:

- While entering a new event in the Add Event screen, tap **Calendars** and then tap the calendar you want to use.

- To add a number of events to a single calendar (for example, your Work calendar), turn off all other calendars so that when you open the Add Event screen, the default is your Work calendar.

- If you are going to be working primarily with one calendar, but don't want to turn off other calendars, you can change the default calendar in Settings. From the Home screen, tap **Settings | Mail, Contacts, Calendars | Default Calendar** and then tap the calendar you want to be the default.

Show Several Calendars Together

With just one calendar, there is no problem finding an event you want to look at, but as soon as you add another calendar, you have to ask the question, "Which calendar do I look at?" The answer, of course, is to superimpose one calendar on the other so you can see them both at the same time. Calendar allows you to do this by simply turning on the calendars you want to display.

1. With Calendar open on your iPhone, tap **Calendars**.

2. Tap the calendars in the Calendars screen that you want to be displayed, as you have seen earlier.

Add Another Calendar

The Calendar app has two types of calendars: those tied to mail accounts (such as Gmail, Outlook, and iCloud) and those created within Calendar. You can, therefore, add calendars from either source. Here's how to add a calendar within Calendar that's not connected with a mail account:

1. From within Calendar, tap **Calendars** to open the Show Calendars screen.

2. Tap **Edit** in the upper-right corner and then tap **Add Calendar** in the approximate middle of the screen.

3. In the Add Calendar screen that opens, type the name of the new calendar and tap the color you want to associate with that calendar.

4. When you are ready, tap **Done**.

To add a calendar from a mail account, follow these steps:

1. Press **Home** to return to the Home screen.

2. Tap **Settings | Mail, Contacts, Calendars** and tap the mail account whose calendar you want to add. The mail account's settings will open. Tap the **On/Off** button to the right of Calendars to turn it on (not all mail servers have calendar services).

3. Press **Home** and tap **Calendar** to return there and eventually see your mail calendar(s).

 NOTE It takes a while before Calendar will see a new mail calendar.

Delete a Calendar

As in adding calendars, you can delete them either from mail accounts or from Calendar itself. You can delete a mail account–related calendar by, in essence, turning it off. Here are the steps to follow:

1. From the Home screen, tap **Settings | Mail, Contacts, Calendars**.

2. Under Accounts, tap the account with an associated calendar that you want to turn off (those with a calendar will say "Calendars").

3. In the mail account details, tap the **On/Off** button to turn it off.

4. Tap **Delete** to confirm that is what you want to do and then tap **Done**.

To delete a calendar created within Calendar, follow these steps:

1. From the Home screen, tap **Calendar | Calendars** in the bottom middle.

2. Tap the right end (the "i" in a circle) of the calendar that you want to delete to open the Edit Calendar screen. You can alternatively tap **Edit** and tap the calendar you want to delete.

3. Scroll to the bottom of the screen, tap **Delete Calendar**, and then tap **Delete Calendar** again to confirm the deletion.

TIP Facebook's calendar is deleted like a mail account's calendar. Tap **Settings | Facebook | Calendar** to turn a Facebook calendar off if it is on, and then tap **Contacts** off to remove Facebook Birthdays.

▷▷ Handle Invitations

Earlier in this chapter you saw how you can add invitations to a new calendar event. When you do that, an invitation is sent to the invitee. If the recipient has a recent iOS device (iPhone, iPad, or iPod touch) and it is set up normally, they will get a notification at the top of their current screen, and the invitation will go directly to the Calendar's inbox. If any of those constraints are not true, the recipient will get an email message with the invitation. Both the Calendar and email invitations provide three links the recipient can click or tap to accept, decline, or maybe accept the invitation.

In an email message there is also an attachment, which you can tap in the Inbox, to open a Calendar event. Tap **Add to Calendar**, select the calendar to use, and tap **Done**. Press

Home to close Mail and then tap **Calendar** to open it and display the event.

Share a Calendar

If several people are working together, sharing a project, have a family in common, or are in an organization together, it can be worthwhile sharing a calendar to better coordinate what they are doing. iPhone's Calendar provides two tools to facilitate this: fully sharing with one or more people a calendar that all can change, and publishing a public calendar that others can subscribe to but only you can change.

Share a Common Calendar

To create a common calendar that two or more people can share with equal ability to add and change events, follow these steps:

1. From the Home screen, tap **Calendar**. Tap **Calendars** and tap the information icon ("i" in a circle) on the calendar you want to share. This opens the Edit Calendar screen.

In a Calendar invitation, tapping **Accept** or **Maybe** creates a calendar event that you can view like any other. With either a calendar or email invitation, accepting, declining, or saying maybe generates information back to the originator in the form of a notification and a Calendar Inbox message.

2. Under Shared With, tap **Add Person** and begin typing the name of the person in your Contacts with whom you want to share this calendar. The person and their email address should pop up. Tap the person to select them.

3. If you want to share with another person, either begin typing a name or tap the plus sign on the right and repeat step 2.

4. When you have added all the people you want, tap **Add** to be shown the Edit Calendar screen, where you can tap **View & Edit** to disallow the other person from editing the calendar or making and changing events.

5. Tap **Done** when you are ready. Upon returning to the Calendars screen, you will see that the calendar you chose to share will now have "Shared With…" under the name of the calendar.

The recipient gets a Calendar notification that you want to share a calendar with them. In their Calendar Inbox they need to tap **Join Calendar** and **Done**. You are then told that they have joined the offered Calendar.

If the recipient taps **Calendar** from the Home screen and then taps **Calendars**, they should see the newly shared calendar in the list of calendars.

The originator will get a notice that the recipient has accepted the invitation.

On a PC, the recipient gets an invitation that looks like other invitations and is able to access the calendar through a link in the invitation to an iCloud PC web app. On a Mac, the recipient gets an invitation and then can look at the calendar in iCal.

Publish a Public Calendar

If you are responsible for a larger public group, such as a Boy or Girl Scout troop, a Little League team, or a book club, and you want to make available a calendar for that organization, you can make a calendar a public calendar that allows anyone to subscribe to it and peruse it. However, they will not be able to change or write to that calendar. To publically share a calendar, follow these steps:

1. In Calendar, tap **Calendars** and tap on the right (the "i" in a circle) of the calendar that you want to make public.

2. In Edit Calendar, tap the **On/Off** button opposite Public Calendar at the bottom to turn it on. This will allow anyone to subscribe to a read-only version of the calendar.

3. After turning on the public calendar, a new option appears: Share Link. Tap this.

4. You are allowed to send the Internet link (URL) for your public calendar to anyone you want using AirDrop, text

messaging, email, Twitter, Facebook, or by copying it to a document, website, or blog. Tap the option you want to use. For example, tap **Mail**, fill in the addressees, and then tap **Send**.

5. When you are done, tap **Cancel**, if needed, and then tap **Done**.

The recipient gets an email, text message, or other invitation, which, when they open it, gives them a very long Internet link. When they tap or click that link, they are asked if they want to subscribe to the public calendar. If they tap or click **Subscribe**, they are told that the calendar has been added, and they can tap or click **View Events** to see it. If you open Calendars, you can also see it.

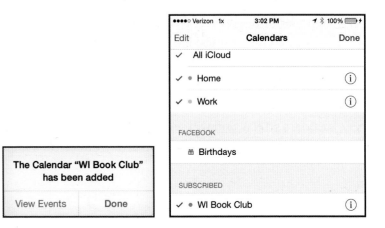

WORK WITH REMINDERS

Reminders is for making lists, to-do lists, shopping lists, and list of steps to complete a project. Reminders may be date and time sensitive and can be marked as completed. They can also remind you that an item has not been completed and can be assigned a priority. Lists can be by date or by list, several of which have been created for you, but you can create as many more as you like. You can sync lists with iCloud and several other products, such as Hotmail's Calendar. If you add a date and time to an item on a list, the item will appear on both the Scheduled and Reminders lists as well as the original list on which you added it.

▷▷ Set Up Reminders

Reminders is very simple. The only setup necessary is the adding, deleting, renaming, and rearranging of lists, and there is only one setting to consider. Here's how set up Reminders:

1. From the Home screen, tap **Reminders**, which will open the app.

2. For general reminders, tap under Reminders twice to open the keyboard and type a reminder. After you have completed the reminder, tap the information icon on the right to open the Details screen for the reminder.

3. If you want to be reminded on a particular day, tap **Remind Me On A Day** and select the date and time. If desired, tap **Repeat** and select the period.

4. If you want to be reminded when you are leaving or arriving at a particular location, tap **Remind Me At A Location** and enter or select the location and then tap **Details**.

5. Tap a priority, enter any desired notes, and when you are ready, tap **Done**.

6. To change a reminder that you have entered, tap the reminder, make any desired text changes, tap the information icon, and make any necessary changes to the details of the reminder. When you are ready, tap **Done**.

7. To delete the reminder or make changes to the list, tap **Edit**, tap the **Do Not Enter** icon, and tap **Delete**. Tap **Done** when you're ready.

8. To add a new list, tap the word **Reminders** at the top of the list, tap **New List**, type a name for the list, pick a color, and tap **Done**.

9. Enter the items on the new list and then tap **Done.**

10. To make changes to a list, tap **Edit** in the top-right area. Tap **Color** and tap a new color to make a change. Tap **Sharing**, tap **Add Person**, begin typing the person's name, select the person's name when it appears, tap **Add**, and tap **Done**.

11. While in Edit mode (see step 10), press and hold on the right end lines ("grip strips") of the list you want to move up or down and then drag it as desired.

12. If you want to delete a list, while in Edit mode, scroll to the bottom of the list and tap **Delete List** and then tap **Delete** to confirm it.

13. Tap **Done** in the top-right area when you have made the changes you want.

14. Review Reminders' settings by pressing the **Home** button and tapping **Settings | Reminders**. Tap **Default List**, tap the list you want other apps outside of Reminders to automatically add to, and tap **Reminders**.

GET TIME AND EVENT INFORMATION

The iPhone provides a number of methods to get information to you, including clocks, alarms, notifications, alerts, and a control center. We'll look at these in three groups: clocks and alarms, notifications and alerts, and the Control Center.

▷▷ Use the Clock and Alarms

The Clock app contains four components: World Clock, Alarm, Stopwatch, and Timer. Tapping **Clock** to open the app displays the last component that you used. If it is not already displayed, tap **World Clock** at the bottom of the Clock screen to begin with that component.

World Clock

World Clock displays a number of clocks for cities around the world. Tap the plus sign in the upper-right corner to add a clock and select the city for it. Tap **Edit**, use the **Do Not Enter** icon on the left to delete a world clock, and use the grip strips on the right to change the order of the clocks. Tap **Done** to complete the editing.

Alarm

The Alarm component allows you to set multiple alarms and turn them on and off as needed. Tap the plus sign in the upper-left corner to add a new alarm. Use the time spinner to select the time the alarm will go off, tap **Repeat** to select the days of the week the alarm will sound, tap **Label** to type a label for the alarm, tap **Sound** to select a sound or a song from your music, and tap **Snooze** to turn that ability on and off. When you have set an alarm, tap **Save**. Once you have an alarm, you can turn it on and off.

Stopwatch

Stopwatch allows you to tap **Start**, tap **Lap** for each lap, and then tap **Stop** to collect a set of times. You can then tap **Reset** to start over.

TIP To save individual times before resetting the stopwatch, take a picture of the iPhone's screen (a "screenshot") by pressing and holding the **On-Off/Sleep-Wake** button while pressing **Home**.

Timer

Timer allows you to set a time in hours and minutes and then tap **Start** to begin a timer for the time you set. You can tap **Pause** to hold the timer until you tap **Resume**. When the timer is finished, you will hear a sound that you can select, and a message will appear on the screen.

▶ Handle Notifications and Alerts

If you have used your iPhone for any time, you have probably seen alerts pop up and notify you about something. They can come from your mail, from your calendar, or from apps you have installed, especially news, sports, and investment publications, as you have seen earlier in this and previous chapters. Alerts generally have self-explanatory buttons—such as OK, View, Close, and Options—that you can tap to carry out that command.

Notifications are another form of alert that repeat their message. Not all notifications have a related alert, but all alerts have a notification. Notifications are in the form of a banner that can be pulled down from the top of the screen by swiping down, usually with a number of other notifications. Tap a banner notification to open the related app and display the item in the notification.

▷▷ Set Up and Use Notifications

The most important aspect of notifications and alerts is the need to control what you get so you get what is important for you and don't get so much it overwhelms you. Notifications and alerts are controlled in Settings.

1. From the Home screen, tap **Settings | Notifications** to open the list of apps in Notifications and other settings.

2. Many (if not most) apps, when they are downloaded and set up, put themselves in Notifications and you get a haphazard list of your apps. The default is the sorting of apps manually, but that means you must do it. Here's how:

   a. Tap **Edit** in the upper-right corner.

   b. Press and hold on the grip strip (lines) to the right of an app you want to move.

   c. Drag the app where you want it in the list.

   d. Repeat steps b and c for all the apps you want to move.

   e. Tap **Done** when you are ready.

3. Each app has several settings within Notifications. As an example, tap **Reminders** (while still under Notifications in Settings).

NOTE Depending on the apps you have downloaded, you may have more or fewer apps than shown here.

a. The first option turns on Reminders in Allow Notifications, the second option lets you determine the number of reminders in Notifications, and the third options lets you select the sound, if any, to be played when the notification appears.

b. You can determine if the app's badge icon (the icon on the Home page) reflects the notification in the form of a number in a red circle and whether the notification appears on the lock screen (the screen you have to swipe from left to right or use your fingerprint to open the iPhone).

c. You have a choice of three styles of alerts:

  - None
  - A banner in Notifications pulled down from the top of the screen
  - Alerts that pop up in the middle of the screen in addition to the banner

4. Repeat step 3 for all the apps whose notification settings you want to change. Some apps have one or more special settings, such as whether to repeat the alert and whom to allow alerts from.

5. When you are ready, return to the Home screen.

NOTE At the bottom of the list of apps in Notifications is an equally important list of apps not in Notifications. For each of these, ask yourself if they are properly categorized.

✔ **QuickFacts**

Using Do Not Disturb

Do Not Disturb, which you can turn on or off from Settings | Do Not Disturb and from the Control Center (the crescent moon icon; see the next section), allows you to silence alerts and incoming FaceTime calls by tapping the **On/Off** button opposite Manual in settings or by tapping the crescent moon icon in the Control Center. If you tap **Do Not Disturb** in Settings, you can do the following:

  - Override the prohibition of alerts for scheduled events by tapping the **On/Off** button opposite Scheduled.
  - Allow calls and FaceTime calls from certain individuals by tapping **Favorites** opposite Allow Calls From and tapping whom to allow.

(Continued)

- Allow calls and FaceTime calls when the call is repeated from the same person within three minutes.

- Choose whether you want calls, FaceTime calls, and notifications silenced when Do Not Disturb is turned on always or only while the iPhone is locked.

When Do Not Disturb is turned on, a crescent moon icon appears to the left of the group of icons on the right at the top of the screen. ◖◢ ✻ 100% ▭ ⚡

⏩ Use the Control Center

The Control Center takes the most heavily used settings and gives you immediate access to them from any screen. You can open the Control Center by swiping up from the bottom of the screen.

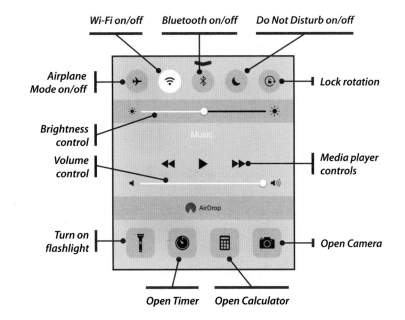

Wi-Fi on/off   Bluetooth on/off   Do Not Disturb on/off

Airplane Mode on/off

Lock rotation

Brightness control

Volume control

Media player controls

Turn on flashlight

Open Camera

Open Timer   Open Calculator

Here are the controls that appear on the Control Center:

- **Airplane mode on/off** Allows you to turn on or off Wi-Fi and Bluetooth, which you might be required to do on an airplane.

- **Wi-Fi on/off** Allows you to turn on or off Wi-Fi.

- **Bluetooth on/off** Allows you to turn on or off Bluetooth, which is used to communicate with accessories such as headphones and keyboards.

- **Do Not Disturb on/off** Allows you to turn on or off the silencing of alerts and incoming FaceTime calls.

- **Lock rotation** Allows you to prevent the screen from rotating when the iPhone is in portrait orientation and you turn it sideways, or if locked when in landscape orientation and you turn it upright.

- **Brightness control** Allows you to set the screen's brightness.

- **Media player controls** Allow you to start and pause playing the currently selected playlist, to go to the beginning of a song (single tap) and the previous song (double-tap), to the next song, and to any point within a song on the bar at the top.

- **Volume control** Allows you to adjust the current volume.

- **AirDrop** Allows you to turn on AirDrop and select whom you receive information from. See "Use AirDrop" later in this chapter.

- **Turn on the flashlight** Allows you to turn on the bright light on the back of the iPhone that is normally used to take pictures.
- **Open Timer app** Allows you to open the Timer app, which includes the clock, alarm, and stopwatch.
- **Calculator** Allows you to open and use the Calculator app as you would any calculator.
- **Open Camera app** Allows you to open the Camera app and take still and video images, as described in Chapter 8.

⊳⊳ Use AirDrop

With AirDrop you can directly share files between two nearby (within 33 feet, or 10 meters) compatible devices (a Mac with OS X Lion or later and an iPhone, iPod, or iPad with iOS 7 or later) without the need for Wi-Fi or cellular. Here's how to use AirDrop:

1. Have two compatible devices within 33 feet of one another.
2. Turn on AirDrop on both devices by opening the Control Center and selecting either **Contacts Only** (if the other device is owned by a contact) or **Everyone**. This makes the devices discoverable by one another.

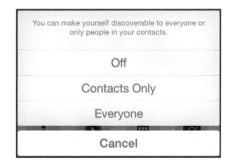

3. In one of the devices, display and select something you want to send to the other device, such as a photo, a document, or a web page. (The selected photos shown next are courtesy of Hank Nelson, Cloudstone Sculpture.)
4. Tap the **Share** icon to open the Share menu. The discoverable devices near you should appear.
5. Tap the device to which you want to send the file or link.
6. On the receiving device, you should see a notice that the other device would like to share a file. If you want to accept it, tap **Accept**.

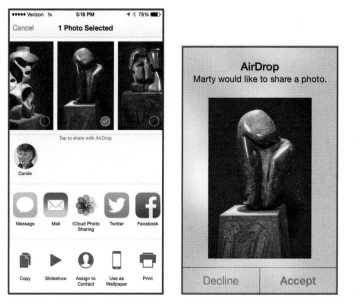

QuickSteps to...

Chapter 6

Taking Photos and Videos

The iPhone is truly a multimedia device. In the next chapter you will see how well it handles literature and music. In this chapter you'll see how it does an equally good job with photos and videos. In addition, you can use it to take and edit photos and videos. We'll look at how to take, edit, and view them on the iPhone as well as how to use FaceTime.

USE THE IPHONE AS A CAMERA

The iPhone has two cameras: the iSight camera on the back and the FaceTime camera on the front. The iSight camera on the iPhone 6 and 6 Plus provides an 8MP (megapixel) stabilized (optical stabilization on the 6 Plus) image with automatic face detection and exposure control, both burst and timer modes, and geotagging to add your current location to a photo. The FaceTime camera provides a 1.2MP stabilized image with many of the same other features. The iPhone provides an excellent alternative to small point-and-shoot cameras.

▷▷ Take Photos

I bet you have already figured out how to take a picture with your iPhone. Regardless, here are the steps:

1. From the Home screen, tap **Camera**. An image of what the camera is looking at will be displayed.

2. Press the shutter button in the middle of the bottom of the screen. That is all there is to it. Your picture will appear at the end of the Camera Roll album.

TIP If you are in a hurry to take a picture, you don't have to unlock your iPhone first; simply swipe up on the camera icon in the lower-right corner of the lock screen to open the Camera app and immediately take a picture.

After taking a couple of pictures with just these two steps, you are going to want to change the focus, zoom in or out, and jump to Photos and jump back to Camera.

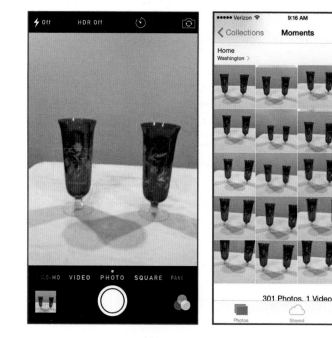

Change Focus and Exposure

The iPhone's cameras have automatic focus and exposure capability. By default, they aim that capability at the center of the image on the screen. They also provide face detection and balance the exposure across up to ten faces. In Camera, when you hold the iPhone still while preparing to take a picture, a yellow square briefly appears on the image showing where the focus is aimed and using a normal or "medium" exposure. As you move the iPhone and change the image, Camera will refocus and the yellow square will briefly reappear to show you what it is focusing on. At any time you can touch the screen to tell the iPhone to focus and set the exposure on that spot. You'll see a smaller yellow square with a sunburst or brightness setting appear where you touched the screen, and face detection will be turned off. You can drag the sunburst up for longer exposure, or down for shorter exposure.

Zoom In or Out

Camera has the standard iPhone zoom capability, where you can zoom in (enlarge the image) by spreading two fingers apart on the screen and zoom out (reduce the image) by bringing two fingers together (pinching) on the screen. When you start to use your fingers to zoom in or out, a slider control appears at the bottom of the screen. You can drag the slider in either direction to accomplish the zooming.

Jump to Photos

As you are taking pictures, you will probably want to quickly look at your latest picture to see if you got what you wanted. You can do that by tapping the thumbnail image of your last snapshot in the lower-left corner. That takes you to the full-screen image of your last photo. Use your finger to scroll from left to right to see previous photos. You can also use any of the Camera Roll controls you learned about earlier in this chapter. If the controls disappear, tap the screen to redisplay them. When you are ready to return to the Camera app, tap **Done** in the upper-right corner.

Use Photo Options

The iPhone provides a number of options for you to use while taking a picture. These include the use of a grid for alignment, a flash in low-light situations, a self-timer to allow you to jump into the photo, and the ability to switch between the front and back cameras.

Use a Grid

As you try to compose a picture, it is sometimes hard to align the object you are photographing within the frame of the picture. To help with that, Camera allows you to turn on a grid that you can use for aligning objects on the screen, as you saw earlier. Turn on or off the grid by tapping **Settings | Photos & Camera | Grid**, as described earlier in the chapter. The grid appears on the screen but will not show up in the photo.

Use the Flash

The iSight camera on the back of the iPhone has a True Tone flash next to it that can be used to add light to your pictures and provide very close to real-life color balance. Control when the flash is used by tapping the lightning bolt icon in the upper-left corner of the screen. This gives you the options of turning the flash on or off, or putting it into automatic mode where the camera senses the need for the flash.

> **TIP** You can use the camera flash as a flashlight when it is dark by turning it on in the Control Center, which you can open by swiping up from the bottom of the iPhone next to the Home button. See the discussion of the Control Center in Chapter 5.

Use the Self-Timer

The self-timer allows you to set up the iPhone camera and then jump into the picture for a "selfie." Set the self-timer by tapping the timer icon in the upper-center-right of the screen and selecting 3S (for three seconds) or 10S (for 10 seconds). Then, when everything is set, tap the shutter button. The iPhone will count down the appropriate number of seconds and then trip the shutter.

Switch from Back to Front

The iPhone has two cameras: one on the back with a higher resolution that is meant for taking the majority of pictures and videos, and one on the front that is primarily for FaceTime conversations or selfies. You can switch between the two by tapping the camera and circular arrows icon in the upper-right corner.

> **TIP** You can find tripods, tripod heads, Bluetooth remote shutter activators, and lens accessories that fit or work with your iPhone at most camera and photography outlets, including Amazon.com.

Take Alternative Types of Photos

In addition to normal photographs, the iPhone can take square, panoramic, HDR (High Dynamic Range), and burst mode photos, as well as apply filters to a photo as you take it.

Take a Square Photo

The normal photo taken by the iPhone is rectangular. iOS gives you the option to make the photo square. In the command bar on the bottom, tap **Square** or drag it to the yellow dot. You will see the elongated sides shorten to form a square. Tap the shutter to take a square photo.

Take a Panoramic Photo

The iPhone with iOS 8 lets you automatically take a series of pictures and stitch them together to create a panoramic picture. In the command bar on the bottom, tap **Pano** or drag it to the yellow dot. You will see an arrow appear, showing the direction to move the camera to capture a panoramic image. Tap the shutter button and move the iPhone in the direction of the arrow. Tap the shutter button again to complete the capture.

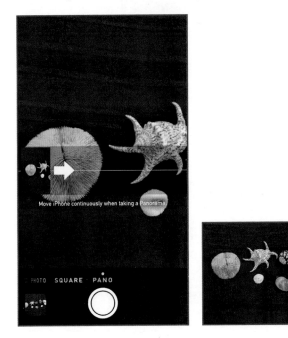

Take an HDR Photo Series

HDR, when it is active, takes three shots, one each at long, short, and normal exposure, and then blends the best parts into a single picture. HDR is particularly useful in situations with extreme contrast and wide variations in lighting. In the top of the screen, tap **HDR** and select **On**, **Off**, or **Auto**. In

Settings, you can choose to keep a normal photo in addition to an HDR one. See "Review Photos & Camera Settings," later in the chapter.

Apply Filters

You can apply various color and monochromatic filters to a photo. Tap the **Filter** icon in the lower-right corner and tap one of the eight filters displayed. Tap the **Filter** icon again to remove the filter choices. Alternatively, you can tap **None** in the center to not have a filter apply. If you want a filter on a picture already taken, you can edit it and apply a filter then. See "Edit Photos," later in this chapter.

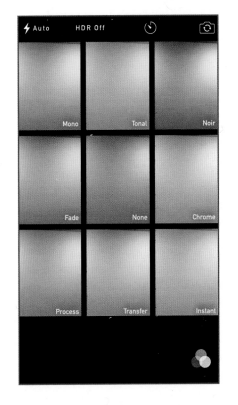

Use Burst Mode

Burst mode allows you to take a quick series of photos and then choose the best one. Touch and hold the shutter button to take a burst of photos. You'll see the counter quickly telling you how many you have taken. To select the photo you want to keep in the burst you have taken, tap the thumbnail in the lower-left corner and tap **Select** in the bottom-middle area. The burst photo set will be shown at the bottom of the screen with one of the sets displayed on the screen. In the set at the bottom, the ones that the iPhone believes to be the best will have a gray dot beneath them and the current one displayed will have a triangle above it. Select a photo you want to keep by tapping the circle in the lower-right corner of the photo displayed on the screen. When you have selected the burst photos you want to keep,

tap **Done**. Then you can delete the remainder of the burst set by displaying it and tapping the delete (trash can) icon.

✓ **QuickFacts**

Moving iPhone Photos to Your Computer

As you take pictures or otherwise collect them on your iPhone, you likely will want them also on your computer. You may be able to do this via iCloud, depending on your use of it, but you can also do this by simply plugging your iPhone into your computer.

Move to a PC

When you plug your iPhone into a PC computer, an AutoPlay message pops up, giving you several options about what to do with your iPhone information. All are good options, but I like to control where information is put on my computer, so I choose **Open Device To View Files** because the other options don't give you the same degree of control. From there, follow these steps:

1. On a PC, in the AutoPlay dialog box, click **Open Device To View Files**. This opens the Windows Explorer (File Explorer on Windows 8) displaying the internal storage of your iPhone.

(Continued)

2. To drill down to your photos, double-click **Internal Storage** to open it. Double-click the **DCIM** file folder to open it, and then double-click the final file folder. This opens the Camera Roll album on your iPhone, displaying the photos it contains, as you see in Figure 6-1.

3. Use the File (Windows) Explorer as you normally would to move the iPhone's photos on the right to folders on your computer on the left.

Move to a Mac

On a Mac, when you plug your iPhone into the computer, iTunes may open it if that is your default setting. Close iTunes, open iPhoto, click your iPhone, click the photos you want to import onto your Mac, and click **Import Selected**, as shown in Figure 6-2. Click either **Delete Originals** or **Keep Originals**. Use the Finder as you normally would to move the iPhone's photos to where you want them.

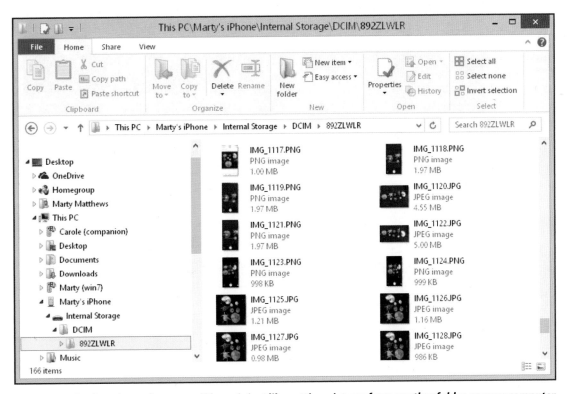

Figure 6-1: Getting photos from your iPhone is just like getting pictures from another folder on your computer.

Figure 6-2: **On a Mac, you need to use iPhoto to initially get photos off the iPhone.**

WORK WITH PHOTOS

There are many reasons why you would want photos on your iPhone: from the simple fact that you like them or want them for the wallpaper on the Home screen, to using them to illustrate points in a document, to display them in a photo essay, or to send to a friend. Whatever the reason, the iPhone makes it easy to acquire, take, edit, store, and use photos. All of these actions are discussed in this section.

▷▷ Use the Photos App

On the iPhone's Home screen, tap **Photos**. A screen of photos should open, as you see on my iPhone next.

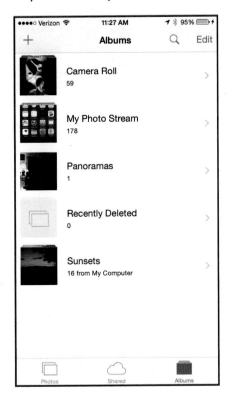

Organize Your Photos

The Photos app provides three primary ways of looking at (or views of) your photos, each of which has further categorization:

- **Photos** Takes all your photos and automatically organizes them into Moments (by date and time), Collections (by location for more recent photos with geocoding), and Years.

- **Shared** If you have set up an iCloud account, Shared displays Shared Streams that contain photos you share with the other devices that are on your iCloud account or are shared with specific people. We'll talk about this later in this chapter in the QuickFacts "Using Photo Stream."

- **Albums** Organizes your photos into groupings called "albums" that you create. For the photos you brought across from your computer, each album is a folder that you had on your computer, as you saw earlier in Figure 6-2. The album named Camera Roll appears when you take pictures with your iPhone's camera or take screen captures. See discussions later in this chapter on taking pictures and capturing screens.

TIP *Screen captures*, or *screenshots*, are images of what is currently on the iPhone's screen. All of the iPhone screen images in this book are screenshots from my iPhone. You take a screenshot by pressing and holding the **On/Off-Sleep/Wake** button while pressing the **Home** button. The screen will go blank for a fraction of a second, and you will hear a "click" sound. The images will go into the Camera Roll album and, if enabled, into your Photo Stream.

Access Your Photos

You can access with your photographs in either the Albums or Photos view. The objective, though, is to get to an individual picture. Here, we'll start with Albums.

1. In the Photos app, if it isn't already selected, tap **Albums** at the bottom-right area of the Photos screen.

2. Tap an album to open it and see and select the photos.

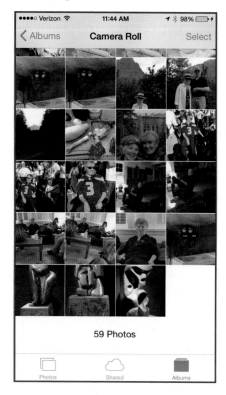

3. Tap a photo to enlarge it. (The photos of sculptures on this page are courtesy of Hank Nelson, Cloudstone Sculpture.)

4. Drag the photo to the left or right to view other photos.

5. Tap a photo to redisplay the controls at the top and bottom.

6. Tap the **Share** icon, select any additional photos in the album by tapping the circle at the bottom of a photo, and tap one of the actions to take with the selected photo(s).

7. When you are ready, tap **Cancel** in the upper-left corner, if you are still in the Share screen, then tap the left arrow in the upper-left corner to close the photo and return to the display of the album's photos. There, you can select another photo or tap **Albums** to return to the album screen. If you actually share a photo in this process, you are returned to the album you were working with.

Work with Albums

As you read earlier, folders on a PC or albums on a Mac that you downloaded from your computer become albums on the iPhone. After you have taken pictures or captured screens, the iPhone creates an album for these items called "Camera Roll." In addition, you can create as many albums as you like. Here's how:

1. To add another album from the album screen, tap the plus sign in the upper-left corner, type an album name, and tap **Save**. In the Photos screen that opens, tap the photos you want to add to the new album. Tap **Done** when you are ready.

2. Tap **Edit** on the far upper-right of the Albums screen. Here you can perform the following actions:

- **Move an album** by dragging the grip strip on the right to where you want the album.

- **Delete** an album that you have created on the iPhone (you can't delete an album that you brought over from your computer) by tapping the **Do Not Enter** icon (a red circle with a white dash in the middle) on the left and then tapping **Delete**.

- **Rename** an album that you have created on the iPhone by tapping the name and using the onscreen keyboard to make the changes you want.

 NOTE You can only rename and delete albums that you create on the iPhone.

3. Tap **Done** when you have completed editing albums.

4. Tap **Photos** to open a screen of your photos and, if needed, go to the Moments display. Tap **Select** and then tap the photos you want to share, delete, or add to other albums.

- Tap the **Share** icon to open the Share menu, where you can attach a photo to a message or email; send it to iCloud, Twitter, Facebook, Pinterest, or Flickr; and copy, print, or perform other actions on it.

- Tap **Add To** to add selected photos to albums that were created on the iPhone. You can't add to albums that you brought over from folders on your computer.

- Tap **Delete** (the trash can) to delete selected images you have taken or copied on your iPhone that don't also exist on your computer or another device. Tap **Delete Photo** to complete the process.

- Tap **Cancel** to stop any operation you have started.

5. Copy a photo by pressing and holding it until the Copy, Hide menu appears. Tap **Copy** and open an album you created on the iPhone. Then either press and hold an existing photo and then tap **Paste** to paste the copy to the left of the existing photo, or press and hold a blank area of the album and tap **Paste** to paste the copy to right of the last existing photo. (The photos of sculptures in the next several examples are courtesy of Hank Nelson, Cloudstone Sculpture.)

Edit Photos

With a single photo displayed, tap **Edit** on the upper-right corner to perform a number of operations:

- Tap **Red-Eye** and tap each eye for which you want to remove red-eye.

- Tap **Enhance** to apply an automatic enhancement, generally brightening.

- Tap **Crop** to open the crop, rotate, and aspect ratio screen. Drag the corners in toward the center to crop the photo on two sides. Tap the rotate icon on the left to rotate the image by 45 degrees, or drag the protractor to any degree of rotation desired. Tap the aspect ratio icon on the right and select a different ratio. Tap **Reset** to return to the original image and tap **Done** when you are finished.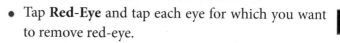

- Tap **Filters** to apply one of eight filters, which you can choose from the option displayed across the bottom of the screen.

- Tap **Color Dial** at the bottom right, and select various degrees of light, color, and black and white.

- Tap **Cancel** to stop whatever editing function is currently underway.

Set Up a Slideshow

A slideshow displays the photos in the current album, one after the other. From the Album view, select a photo, tap the **Share** icon, and tap **Slideshow** to create one. The Slideshow Options menu will open. See "Review Photos & Camera Settings," later in this chapter.

- Tap **Transitions** and review the various transitions available. Try several to see which one you like and then use it.

- If desired, tap the **Play Music** on/off switch, tap **Music**, and then select the piece you want to play in the background.

- Tap **Start Slideshow** to start your new slideshow.

Using Photo Stream

Photo Stream is a component of iCloud that allows you to share recent photos that you have taken on your iPhone with other devices that share your iCloud account. Of course, you must have set up and enabled an iCloud account, as described in Chapter 1. Also, Photo Stream must be enabled in Settings, as described in "Review Photos & Camera Settings," later in this chapter.

Photos you take with Camera or screenshots (see the Tip earlier in this chapter near the "Access Your Photos" section) you capture on your iPhone go into the Camera Roll album. They are automatically uploaded to your Photo Stream on iCloud, if it is enabled, after you leave Camera. The photos can then be viewed on all the devices that share your iCloud account, including PC and Mac computers. On your iPhone you will also see photos taken or captured on your other iCloud-enabled devices. You can keep up to 1,000 photos on your Photo Stream, and they won't count against your total iCloud storage.

It's easy to manage your Photo Stream:

1. From the Home screen, tap **Photos** (if necessary), return to Albums, tap **My Photo Stream**, and tap **Select** on the top right.

2. Tap the photo(s) you want to share, delete, or save to your iPhone.

3. Tap the **Share** icon in the bottom-left corner to open the Share menu and add the photo(s) to a message, an email, iCloud

Photo Sharing (see the next section), or Facebook (or that you want to copy, print, or perform other actions on), as you have seen earlier in this chapter.

4. Tap **Add To** to save the selected photo(s) to an existing album that you have created or to a new album.

5. Tap **Delete** (the trash can) to remove the selected photo(s) from your Photo Stream on your iPhone. This does not delete the original photo(s).

iCloud Photo Sharing

iCloud Photo Sharing is a separate album you share with other people not on your iCloud account but who have iOS 6 or later or OS X Mountain Lion or later devices (recent iPhone, iPad, and iPod touch devices as well as Macs). Here's how to create an iCloud Photo Sharing album:

1. In Settings | Photos & Cameras, turn on iCloud Photo Sharing, if it isn't already on (see "Review Photos & Camera Settings," later in this chapter).

2. From most Photos screens, tap **Shared** at the bottom of the screen to open iCloud Photo Sharing.

3. Tap the plus sign in the upper-left corner to open and name a new stream you are creating.

4. Tap **Next** and enter the email address of someone you want to share your new stream with. Tap the plus sign in a circle to enter additional email addresses to share your stream with more people.

(Continued)

5. When you are ready, tap **Create.**

6. Tap the new stream and tap the plus sign to open Photos. Tap the photos you want to include in your new photo stream, tap **Done**, and tap **Post**. The new folder will open and display the selected photos.

7. Tap **People** at the bottom of the screen to invite additional people and decide how you want to manage the photo stream.

The people you have invited will receive an email message asking if they want to subscribe to your photo stream.

Review Photos & Camera Settings

The following settings are available for Photos; from the Home screen, tap **Settings | Photos & Camera:**

- **iCloud Photo Library** allows you to turn on or off the automatic uploading of your entire photo library to iCloud so you can access this library on any iOS device using your iCloud ID and password.

- **My Photo Stream** allows you to turn on or off the basic Photo Stream capability. See the "Using Photo Stream" QuickFacts.

- **Upload Burst Photos** allows you to turn on or off a fast sequence of photos that can be up to 10 frames per second.

- **iCloud Photo Sharing** allows you to turn on or off the Shared Photo Stream capability. See the "Using Photo Stream" QuickFacts.

- **Summarize Photos** allows you to choose a compact summarized view for Collections and Years.

- **Play Each Slide For** allows you to set the number of seconds (from 2 to 20) for which each slide plays in a slideshow.

- **Repeat** allows you to turn on or off the playing of a slideshow.

- **Shuffle** allows you to turn on or off the random mixing of slides in a slideshow.

- **Grid** allows you to turn on or off a grid for better aligning a photo. This does not show in the final picture.

- **Record Video At 60 FPS** allows you to turn on or off the ability to take high-speed video at 60 fps (frames per second).

- **Keep Normal Photo** saves a normal photo when an HDR (High Dynamic Range) series of photos is taken that blends the best parts of three separate exposures.

WORK WITH VIDEOS

Your iPhone provides an excellent way to record, edit, and even watch videos. The iPhones 6 and 6 Plus allow you to record 1,080-pixel high-definition (HD) video at either 30 fps or 60 fps. You can also record slow-motion video at either 120 fps or 240 fps, as well as time-lapse video. This makes the iPhone a good video-recording device. With the iPhone's cameras, you can record videos in much the same way as you take a photo, do some limited editing with the default apps, and download apps for more comprehensive video editing. You can also download movies and TV shows and watch them on the iPhone. Although the iPhone has a small screen, if you are the only one watching it and you use the EarPods to listen, it is not a bad experience, especially on an airplane.

⊳⊳ Download Videos

There is an almost unlimited number of videos you can view on your iPhone. This includes movies, TV shows, music and personal videos, and video podcasts. You can download videos from iTunes and many additional sources on the Internet. When you download a video, you may have it permanently, although in the cases of rentals and library loans, what you downloaded will disappear after a set time. You can also *stream* a video, which means that it is sent to you in small bites as you view it. Streaming, though, requires that you have a faster, stable Internet connection. Look at what is available and how to use videos from the iTunes Store and then look at what else is available.

CAUTION! Full-length movies are large files in the range of 3GB to 4GB. They take a good amount of time to download; require stable, fast Internet and Wi-Fi connections; and if you use cellular, they will take a fair bite out of your data plan. They can also use up the iPhone's memory pretty fast.

Download from iTunes

Using iTunes on your iPhone to get videos is similar to using it to get books and music, although it takes a lot longer.

1. From the Home screen, tap the **iTunes Store** icon and on the bottom menu bar toward the left, tap **Movies** to see a number of movies displayed.

2. See additional videos within an individual category, generally listed in a row, by swiping it to the left. See additional categories by swiping up.

3. Tap a video to see additional information and view trailers of it. Tap a trailer to view it.

TIP For many movies on iTunes, you can choose to rent or buy them. If you buy a movie, you can permanently keep it and watch it as many times as you wish. If you rent a movie, you have 30 days to begin watching it and then 24 hours to finish watching it (in the USA; 48 hours elsewhere) from the time you click Play.

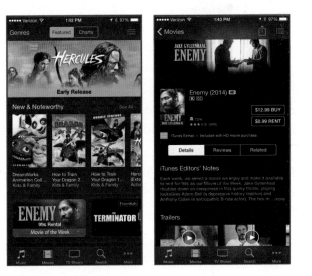

4. Tap either the **Buy** price or the **Rent** price (if it is available) and then select **HD** (high definition and a large file size) or **SD** (standard definition and a much smaller file size). Tap **Buy Movie** (or **Buy Video**) or **Rent Movie**, enter your Apple ID password, possibly verify your credit card, and then tap **OK** to complete the process. You will see the downloading icon where the amount was. If you tap **Downloads** in the lower-right corner, you will see 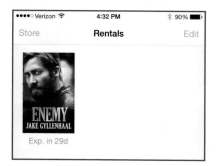 the progress of the downloading.

5. Tap outside of the information box to close the added information.

6. When the downloading has finished, press **Home**, tap **Videos**, and tap your video to play it. If you rented a video, you will be told the number of days you have left.

▷▷ Make Videos

The iPhone's cameras make videos as well as photos, and you make a video very much like you do a photo. Normal video is taken at 30 fps, but in Settings | Photo & Camera, you can change this to 60 fps (see "Review Photos & Camera Settings," earlier in this chapter).

1. On the Home screen, tap **Camera** and then tap or drag the **Video** option over to the yellow mark on the screen.

2. Aim the camera where you want to begin the video capture, press the red button at the bottom center, and then pan the iPhone (move it from left to right or from right to left) to capture what you want in the video. A timer at the top of the screen shows you how long you have been shooting.

TIP While you are shooting a video, you can take a still photograph by pressing the shutter button in the bottom-left corner.

3. When you are done capturing, press the red square button that has replaced the red round button in the bottom center. You can then view what you just shot by tapping the thumbnail of your video at the bottom right.

4. Tap the triangle in the middle of the screen to play the video. Videos you produce are kept in Photos, not in Videos, but in the Videos album.

5. You can start playing a video at any place during its duration by tapping in the sequence of frames at the top of the screen, or you can drag a finger across the frames to quickly or slowly view the video.

TIP You can take a screenshot of a particular frame in the video and in this way you can identify the best photo in the sequence of action.

▷▷ Edit and Share Videos

As you take videos, you may notice that you have frames at either the beginning or end of the video that you want to remove. The iPhone provides a simple video editor that lets you trim frames from either end of a video clip, but not remove frames from the middle of it. You can also delete a video or share it with others in various ways.

1. From the Home screen, tap **Photos**, tap **Albums** (if needed), tap **Videos** or the album you are using for your videos, and tap the video you want to work with. It will open and have the features you saw at the end of the last section. If you don't see the series of frames at the top of the screen, tap the video.

2. To trim an end off the selected video, tap either end of the series of frames so it becomes enclosed in a yellow border. Drag toward the middle from either end until the frames you want to trim have become dim. Tap **Trim** in the upper-right corner and then tap either **Trim Original**, so you only have a clip without the frames you trimmed, or **Save As New Clip**, to create a new clip without the trimmed frames and still have the original clip with the frames.

3. To delete the entire video, tap the recycle bin in the lower-right corner and then tap **Delete Video**.

4. To share a video with other people, tap the **Share** icon in the lower-left corner of the screen and then tap the method (Message or Mail) or service (YouTube, Facebook, or Vimeo) you want to use. Note that YouTube and Vimeo are unique to videos. In both cases, you must have an existing account to upload videos.

TIP Apple offers for free a very capable video-editing app called iMovie, which you can download and use from the App Store.

Take Time-Lapse and Slow-Motion Video

The iPhone 6 and 6 Plus offer both time-lapse and slow-motion video. In Camera, tap **Time-Lapse** and then tap the shutter button. The iPhone will take a still photo about every seven seconds, until you tap the shutter again. It will then put the still photos together into a video that you can edit as such. For slow-motion, in Camera tap **Slo-Mo** at the bottom of the screen and then tap the speed, either 120 fps or 240 fps. Tap the shutter to start the video and then tap it again when you are done. If you select the slow-motion video in Photos, you will see a time bar beneath the video frames. You can drag the two black vertical bars, representing the start and end of the slow-motion segment, anywhere within the time bar to indicate the part you want in slow motion.

USE FACETIME

FaceTime makes the iPhone (or an iPad or iPod touch) into a video phone, where you can contact someone and have a face-to-face conversation with them—in other words, a video chat. To use FaceTime, you need to have an Apple ID and either a Wi-Fi or cellular connection to the Internet. Note, however, that in using a cellular service for FaceTime you may incur data charges.

Here's how to make a FaceTime call:

1. Tap the **FaceTime** icon on the Home screen. The FaceTime screen will appear with some of your contacts.

2. Tap the person in your contact list that you want to call. An intermediate screen will appear showing who you are

calling and giving you controls to switch the front and back camera, disconnect the call (hang up), and mute the call.

3. When the other person answers, they will appear on your screen with your picture inset in a corner. You can begin talking as you normally would. The iPhone's microphone is pretty good, and you shouldn't have to lean in.

4. Drag the small image of you to any of the four corners.

5. When you are done with the call, tap the screen and then tap **Disconnect** (the red dot with a handset).

6. You can show the person you are talking to what you are looking at by tapping the **switch camera** icon, on the left, to activate the other camera in the iPhone and then aiming the iPhone at what you want to show.

7. You can also mute the iPhone's microphone—if, for example, you want to take a call on another phone—by tapping the **mute** icon.

8. If you want to resume a FaceTime call, tap **Recents** and then tap the call you want to resume.

Chapter 7

Listening to and Reading on the iPhone

In the first six chapters, I've primarily covered how to get the most productive use out of your iPhone. In this chapter, you'll see how to relax and enjoy your iPhone by locating, getting, organizing, and listening to music and then how to locate, organize, and read electronic books (ebooks) and other documents.

LISTEN TO MUSIC

Music has always been a powerful part of human history, and it remains so in this mobile digital age. People may not agree on the type of music they like, but the majority of people like to listen to some form of it—and the iPhone supports that in spades. Here, we'll look at getting music from two sources (iTunes and your computer), organizing it into playlists, and then listening to it.

▷▷ Get Music from iTunes

iTunes makes available for purchase and download over 37 million songs. iTunes is easy to use to search, open, preview, and buy music that you want to listen to.

> **TIP** In addition to music, at the iTunes Store you can buy movies, TV shows, and other media. The general discussion here on how to use iTunes applies equally to all the types of media available through it. I talked briefly about getting videos and movies in Chapter 6.

Set Up iTunes

iTunes comes already installed on the iPhone, and using it requires little more than opening it. You must, of course, have an Apple ID, but you most likely have that, as described in Chapter 1. Take a brief look at the iTunes settings by tapping **Settings | iTunes & App Stores** from the Home screen:

- **Show All** allows you to determine whether you want to show all of the music and videos you have purchased from iTunes and in iTunes Matches (see next item) as well as whether you have downloaded them to your iPhone. The default is to show them.

- **iTunes Match** allows you to subscribe (for $24.99 a year) to an iCloud service that stores all of your music, regardless of whether you bought it on iTunes or not.

- The four **Automatic Downloads** options allow purchases on other devices, such as an iPad, to be automatically downloaded to your iPhone. These are on by default, and under most circumstances, you want to leave them that way.

- If you have a limited data plan, you probably do *not* want to use cellular for the automatic downloads between Apple devices and for iTunes Match. This is the default, which you probably want to leave.

- **Suggested Apps** allows you to turn on or off the suggestions on the lock screen and App Switcher of apps that you have installed or are available from the App Store related to your current location. The default is that they are both turned on.

Become Familiar with iTunes

Take a quick look around iTunes and get familiar with the interface. Open it by tapping **iTunes Store** on the Home screen. The iTunes screen that opens has two sets of selectors. At the bottom of the screen are the primary categories of Music, Movies, TV Shows, Search, and More. For each of the first three categories at the bottom there is a set of genres, or subcategories, available by tapping **Genres** at the top-left area of the screen.

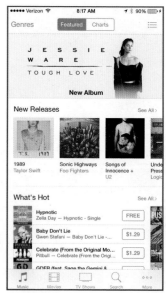

The last two items on the bottom allow you to search iTunes or open five additional sources of music. At the top of the screen, in addition to selecting a list of genres, you can choose between Featured, pieces selected by iTunes (the default), and Charts, pieces selected based on their popularity. Within Charts you can see the most popular singles at the top, followed by albums and music videos. On both the Featured and Charts screens, you can scroll most rows from right to left.

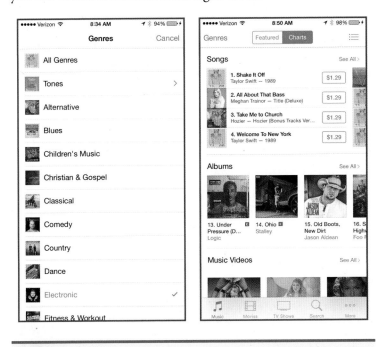

NOTE As seniors, we may not recognize much of the music that is displayed, but iTunes has our music also.

Search iTunes

The key hurdle in using iTunes, of course, is finding the music you want to buy. iTunes gives you several ways of reviewing what is available.

1. When you first open iTunes, All Genres is selected on the Genres screen. This provides a smattering of recent popular albums and songs of different types.

2. To hone in on a particular genre, tap **Genres** at the top-left corner to review what is available.

3. Tap several genres that appeal to you, such as Blues, Classical, Jazz, Pop, and Rock, and look at what is available.

4. Tap **Search** in the bottom-right area to open the Search box at the top of the screen, where you can enter album, artist, and composer names, as well as categories of music. For example, to search for the music of my youth and young adulthood, I entered **Music of the 50s and 60s** and was amazed at all I got.

TIP Don't limit your searches to albums or artists. Try any unique categories you might think of.

Preview and Buy Music

Once you have found the music you may want, the next step is to preview it and make sure it is what you really want—and, if so, to buy it. To preview and potentially buy an album or song that you have found, follow these steps:

1. From the iTunes page you found earlier—for example, the result of my "Music of the 50s and 60s" search—tap an album or song you are interested in. I tapped **Cruisin' to the Hits of the '50s and '60s**.

2. You get an overview, review summary, price, and list of the songs on the album or just the individual song. Tap any of the songs to have a 90-second preview of it played on your iPhone.

3. When you find a song or album that you want to buy, tap the price, tap **Buy Song**, BUY SONG use your Touch ID or enter your Apple ID password, and tap **OK**. You will see your song downloading, and when it is done, the word "Play" replaces the price. PLAY The first time you buy something from the iTunes or App Store, you will be asked to agree to Apple's terms of sale (a 34-page document you can have emailed to you). You are asked this even if the app or song you are getting is free.

▷▷ Transfer Music from a Computer

If you have had a computer for any length of time, you probably have put some music on it, either by downloading the music or by copying CDs you have to your computer (called "ripping" CDs). The major way to get music from other iTunes sources to your iPhone is through your computer, and to do that you need to have iTunes installed on your computer. You may already have iTunes on your computer, but if not return to Chapter 1 and install it now; then look at collecting the music you have on your computer, ripping CDs to iTunes, and finally transferring and syncing your music between your computer and your iPhone.

Collect the Music on Your Computer

To get the music from your computer onto your iPhone, it must first reside in iTunes on your computer. In many instances iTunes will automatically find and list the music from your computer if it is in the standard folders, and you will not need to do anything more (see Figure 7-1).

If iTunes did not automatically locate and list your music, assist it by opening the file system on your computer (Windows or File Explorer on Windows, or Finder on a Mac) and locating

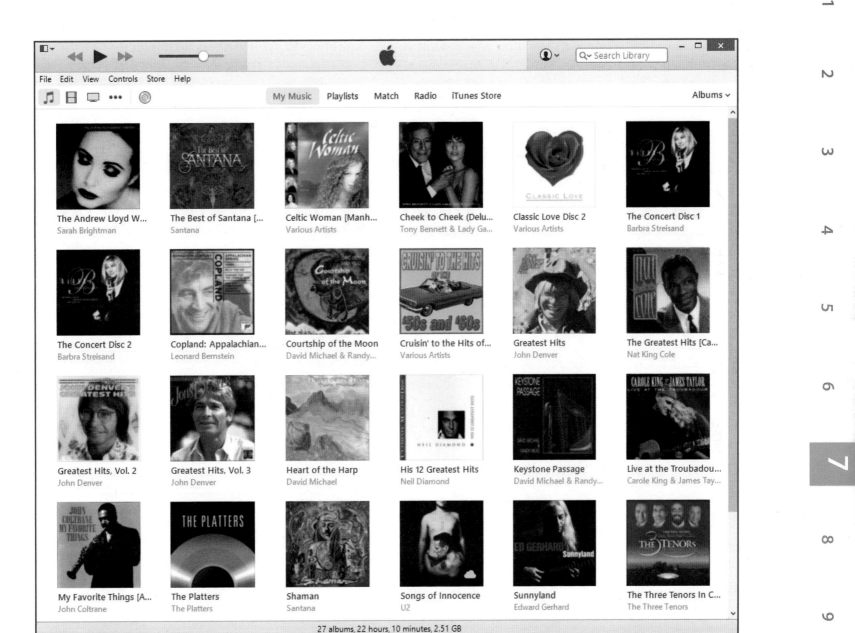

Figure 7-1: iTunes is more than a conduit for communicating between your iPhone and your computer; it is also a great organizer and player of music on your computer.

your music. On recent Windows computers (7 and 8), it is probably located within Libraries/Music/. On Macs (recent OS X versions), it is probably located within Music. With that knowledge, follow these steps:

1. In iTunes on your computer, the first time you use it, click **Scan For Media**. This will pick up the easily recognized music. On my computer it picked up most of the 27 albums I have.

2. Still in iTunes on your computer, click **File | Add Folder To Library**. Navigate to the folder that contains any music not automatically picked up.

3. Click the top album, press and hold SHIFT, click the bottom album to select them all, and click **Select Folder**.

4. You may be told that one or more of the songs you are adding to iTunes needs to be converted to a different format. Click **Convert**. The process of converting and adding your music to iTunes may take several minutes, depending on how big your library is.

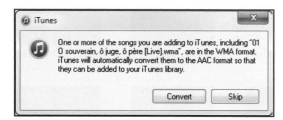

Rip CDs to iTunes

Here's how to rip or add music from a CD to iTunes:

1. If it isn't already, start iTunes on your computer.

2. Place the CD in your computer's CD drive. iTunes will open, displaying the CD you inserted and its songs.

3. iTunes will ask if you want to import the CD. Click **Yes**.

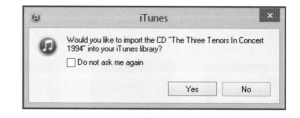

 TIP If you don't want to import the entire CD, you can uncheck the songs you do not want to import.

4. If you are asked about import settings, unless you have a special need, accept the default and click **OK**.

5. As the CD is being imported, you'll see the status at the top and a green check mark in a green circle.

6. If you are told that the cover artwork cannot be found, click **OK**. You can live without it or come back later and try to find it (do an Internet search on the title).

7. When you are done importing, remove the CD from the computer.

Transfer and Sync to iPhone

You can transfer all or selected parts of the music on your computer to your iPhone automatically by syncing it, in essence making the music on your iPhone the same as the music on your computer.

1. Plug your iPhone into a Universal Serial Bus (USB) port on your computer and unlock the iPhone, if necessary.

2. On your computer, start iTunes, click your iPhone in the objects bar (it should be the object on the left but closest to the center), and click **Music** under Settings, as you can see in Figure 7-2.

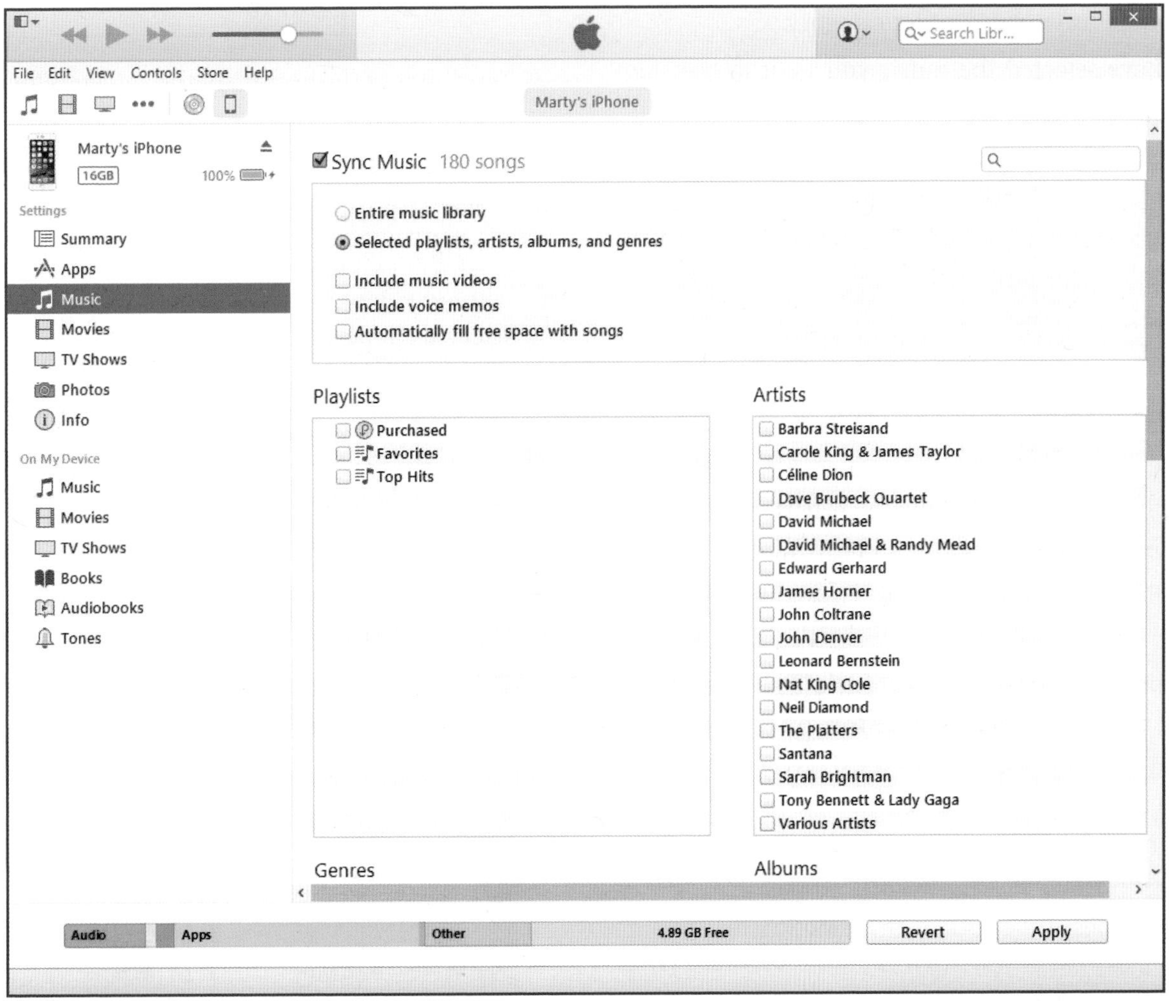

Figure 7-2: *iTunes on your computer allows you to have consistent music on both your computer and your iPhone.*

3. Click **Sync Music** and click either **Entire Music Library** or **Selected Playlists**. I recommend Selected Playlists to conserve space on the iPhone.

4. Review the playlists, artists, genres, and albums and select (check) the ones you want on your iPhone. Note that the lists duplicate each other. Probably the least confusing is to select albums and not any other category.

5. When you have selected the music you want to transfer, click **Apply** in the lower-right corner.

Syncing transfers the music that is not currently on your iPhone from your computer to the iPhone, but the opposite is not true—music that's on the iPhone but not on the computer will not be transferred to the computer.

Syncing Music to "Marty's iPhone" (Step 5 of 5)
Copying 11 of 161: It's Too Late

▷▷ Create Playlists

A playlist is a list of songs from various albums that you want to play together in sequence. Selecting the playlist plays all the songs on it. The process of creating a playlist entails simply selecting the songs you want on the list and giving it a name. Here is how you do it in the iPhone's Music app:

1. From the iPhone's Home screen, tap **Music | Playlists** on the bottom left. If you see Playlists, tap **More** on the right and then tap **Playlists**. If you have purchased several individual songs on an album, they will be shown as a playlist under the album's name.

NOTE The icons at the bottom of the Music screen can be rearranged according to what you use most often by tapping **More | Edit** and dragging the icons to where you want them.

2. To create a new playlist, tap **New Playlist** (the plus sign), type a name, and tap **Save**.

3. Tap **Songs** at the bottom of the screen. This will open a list of all the songs on all the albums you have either imported from your computer or purchased on iTunes.

4. Either swipe up or use the alphabetic index on the far right to scroll through the list so you can find the songs you want.

5. Tap the songs you want on the playlist. When you have selected all the songs you want, tap **Done**. The list of songs on your playlist will appear.

6. Tap **Edit** in the upper left to go into edit mode.

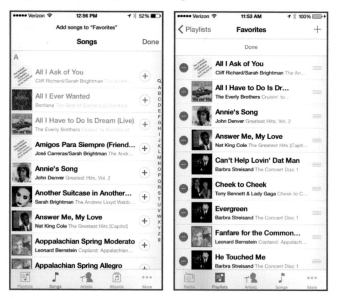

7. To delete a song on the list, tap the white bar in the red circle and then tap **Remove**. Drag the grip strip on the far right to reposition songs within the list.

8. To add a song to the list, tap the plus sign in the upper right and repeat steps 3 through 5. When the list is the way you want it, tap **Playlists** on the left. Your new playlist will appear on Music's Playlists page.

Listen to Music

You can listen to music on your iPhone using iPhone's Music app, which has a number of features to fulfill that function. Unless it has been moved, the Music icon is on the right end of the dock at the bottom of the Home screen.

To play music on your iPhone from the Home screen, tap **Music**, tap one of the categories at the bottom, tap **Radio**, **Playlists**, **Songs**, **Artists**, or **More** where you find Albums, Genres, Compilations, and Composers, and finally tap an

individual song you want to play. The iPhone's player will open with these controls:

Return to library — Song list — Album cover — Progress bar — Current position — Play/Pause — Previous track — Next track — Volume slider

- **Return to library** (the arrow in the upper-left corner) leaves the current song and returns to the Playlist, Album, or Artist library, but leaves the song playing unless you pause it.

- The **song list** (the three lines in the upper-right corner) displays the list of songs in the album.

●●●●○ Verizon 🌐	4:39 PM	🔋 ✳ 100% 🔋 ⚡

Rating   Done

| Album | Playlist |

Sarah Brightman
The Andrew Lloyd Webber Co...
16 songs
1:06:20

1	The Phantom of the Opera	4:22
2	Unexpected Song	2:57
3	Aspects of Love [From Chanson d'E...	3:56
📶	All I Ask of You	4:11
5	Don't Cry for Me Argentina	5:55
6	Another Suitcase in Another Hall	3:22
7	Aspects of Love [From Love Change...	3:35
8	Amigos Para Siempre (Friends for Li...	4:37
9	Memory	3:59
10	Gus: The Theatre Cat	5:12

- The **current position** shows where you are currently in the song that is playing. You can drag the red position marker (also called a "Playhead") in either direction to move what is currently playing.

- The **progress bar** provides the span for marking the current position in a song that is playing. The number of minutes already played and remaining are at either end of the progress bar.

- **Player controls** with Previous and Next allow you to step through an album one track at a time in either direction, and Play and Pause allow you to start and stop playing the current song.

- The **volume slider** can be dragged left or right to lower or raise the volume of the music being played.

- **Repeat** repeats the current song.

- **Create** allows you to create a new playlist or radio station based on the currently selected artist or song.

- **Shuffle** rearranges the list of songs in an album and plays them in a random order.

TIP To delete an album from your iPhone, tap **More | Albums** (unless you have rearranged the icons), swipe the album from right to left, and tap **Delete**. You cannot delete albums that are on iCloud (for example, the free U2 album Apple gave everyone). To remove it from your iPhone, in Safari go to itunes.com/soi-remove, tap **Remove Album**, sign in with your ID and password, and you will be told the album is removed.

Control Music

Actually controlling the music you are playing is, at this point, anticlimactic, and you probably have, with the touch controls so obvious, figured it out. This, of course, varies a bit, depending on the view you have on the screen.

1. After tapping the song you want to play, the player will open with the progress bar, player controls, and volume slider, as described previously, and the song will begin. The entire playlist, album, or artist collection will play if you don't interrupt it.

2. Tap **Pause** in the player controls to temporarily stop playing the music. Tap **Play** to start playing again where you left off.

3. Tap **Previous** or **Next** to go to the previous or next song or track in the album.

4. Drag the volume slider to increase or decrease the volume.

 TIP Some headphones, such as Apple's EarPods, which can be plugged in on the left of the Lightning USB cable, allow you to adjust the volume remotely on the wire to the headphones.

Set Up Music

Open Music's settings from the Home screen by tapping **Settings | Music**. Options include the following:

●●●●● Verizon 🗑	6:53 PM	🗲 ✻ 100% 🔋✚
❮ Settings	**Music**	
Shake to Shuffle		⬭
Sound Check		⬭
EQ		Off ›
Volume Limit		Off ›
Lyrics & Podcast Info		🔵
Group By Album Artist		🔵
Show All Music		🔵
All music that has been downloaded or that is stored in iCloud will be shown.		
Genius		⬭
Turning on Genius will share information about your music library anonymously with Apple. Learn More		
Subscribe to iTunes Match		
Store all your music in iCloud and listen to music on		

- **Shake To Shuffle** lets you shake your iPhone to change the order in which songs are played.
- **Sound Check**, when turned on, levels out volume highs and lows.
- **EQ** allows you to select preset equalizer settings for various types of music.

- **Volume Limit** lets you set a maximum volume limit, which you might want to use with headphones.
- **Lyrics & Podcast Info** provides added information when it is available.
- **Group By Album Artist** groups albums by one artist together.
- **Show All Music** provides for the display of all music that has been downloaded to the iPhone or stored on your iCloud account.
- **Genius** allows Apple to anonymously gather information about your music library so they can suggest similar music to you.
- **iTunes Match** sets up the storing of all of your music on iCloud, including music you have ripped from CDs and downloaded from other sources. See "Set Up iTunes" earlier in this chapter.
- **Home Sharing** displays the Apple ID used with Home Sharing.

 TIP Turning the iPhone to Landscape orientation (lengthwise) displays a full screen of your album covers.

Use the Control Center Controls

If you are playing music while also using another app, such as an app for reading a book or magazine, you can quickly get to a set of player controls in the Control Center without having to open the Music app and possibly losing your place in what you are reading.

You can display the audio controls from any open screen on your iPhone by swiping up from the bottom of the screen and using the same player controls described earlier.

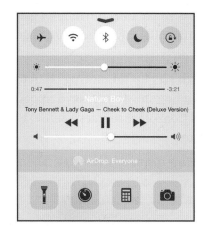

Listen to iTunes Radio

iTunes Radio is a competitor of Pandora and other streaming Internet "radio" stations (where the music is sent to you as you are listening to it). iTunes Radio provides a number of stations either dedicated to particular types or genres of music or groupings of music such as the current top 50 songs or The Beatles Radio. You can also create your own station, which is stored on iCloud, so you can listen to it and any of the other stations anywhere you have iTunes, including your iPhone, iPad, iPod, and your PC or Mac computer.

NOTE iTunes Radio is itself free, but there will be occasional ads to listen to, and you are reminded that you can buy the current song for your own library by clicking the price associated with it. If you sign up for iTunes Match (explained earlier in this chapter), you will be spared the advertising.

If you have never used iTunes Radio, you may not see the icon at the bottom of the Music screen and you will need to download the app from the App Store. Tap **App Store** and tap **Search** on the bottom right of the screen. Tap in the Search box at the top of the screen, type **itunes radio**, and tap **Search**. When iTunes Radio appears, tap **Listen Now**.

If you do see the iTunes Radio icon at the bottom left of the Music screen, tap it. In either case, iTunes Radio will open. Across the top are featured stations, and on the bottom is space for your own selected ones. To use iTunes Radio on your iPhone, follow these steps:

1. Scroll Featured Stations by swiping from right to left.
2. Select a station to listen to by tapping it. The Now Playing screen will open and display the album cover for the current song, as well as the familiar player controls.

3. Tap the info icon for more information about the current song and to create a new station based on the current artist or current song. You can also tune the current station to play only the top hits or a variety of related music, or you can explore some variations of the theme of the current station. Finally, you can choose to allow explicit tracks as well as if and how you want to share this station with others.

4. There are several ways to start a station of your own. As you read in step 3, you can start a new station based on an artist or a song you are currently playing. You can also tap **New Station** (the red plus sign) on the iTunes Radio page and select a genre and possibly a subcategory. Finally, you can use the search box at the top of the screen and enter an artist, song, or genre.

TIP If you only have one of your own radio stations, you can see the New Station plus sign on the initial iTunes Radio screen. If you have two or more of your own stations, you will need to scroll up from bottom to top to see New Station.

5. To change or delete a radio station you have created, tap **Edit** on the left of the My Stations heading. Tap the station you want to work with. You can add artists, songs, and/ or genres that you want more of or don't want to hear. Alternatively, you can tap **Delete Station** and then tap **Delete** to remove the station.

READ ON THE IPHONE

Reading on the iPhone is easy, and the iPhone offers a lot to read. Many newspapers are available both in Safari and in their own apps. Also, a large number of magazines, again both online and in their own apps, are available. Then there is the iBook app that comes with iPhone with which you can buy books and read them. Finally, several third-party ebook readers are available in the App Store, along with thousands of free books that you can read, and a great number more that you can buy.

Read Using Safari

A great deal of material to read on the Internet is available directly in Safari without another app, as you have seen in Chapter 3. This includes web pages themselves, blogs (web logs, or ongoing writing about a particular subject), newspapers, and magazines. To read on Safari (for example, *The New York Times* website), follow these steps:

1. From the Home screen, tap **Safari**.

2. Tap in the address box at the top center of the screen and then tap the **X** on the right end of the box to remove its contents.

3. Type **nytimes.com** and tap **Go**. *The New York Times* home page will open.

4. When you see an article you want to read, tap it to open a page with that story.

5. Tap **Reader** (the stack of lines) at the left end of the address bar. The article will appear in a well-formatted, easy-to-read page.

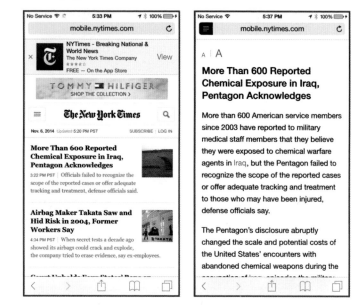

▷▷ Read Using the Newsstand

The Newsstand is a holder for certain newspapers and magazines whose app has been customized so that the publication goes into the Newsstand (the Newsstand itself is not an app). One such magazine is *National Geographic.* Here's how to get and use it:

1. From the Home screen, tap the **Newsstand** icon to open the Newsstand.

2. Tap **Store** on the bottom-right corner of the Newsstand. The App Store will open and display several magazines.

3. To locate a magazine you don't immediately see, tap and clear the search box in the upper-right corner, type the magazine name, and tap **Search**. A set of magazine apps will appear.

4. Tap **National Geographic** in either the original set of magazines, if it appeared in step 2, or as a result of the search in step 3.

5. Tap **Free**, tap **Install**, and then tap **Open**. A page opens showing recent copies of the magazine, where you can buy individual issues or subscribe for a year.

6. Tap your choice, tap **Buy**, type your Apple ID password, and tap **OK**. Tap **Download**. The magazine will download and then be displayed.

TIP Some magazines automatically download new issues and sometimes automatically charge you for that new issue, depending on your subscription arrangement with them. By tapping **Settings | iTunes & App Store**, you can turn off the Automatic Downloads Updates.

Read Using iBooks

With iBooks, you can carry a small library around with you; add to that the iBookstore and the iCloud, and you have an endless supply of reading material. The iBooks app is not only a container and organizer for your books, as is Newsstand for magazines, but it is also a reader, a portal to the iBookstore, and a means to fully annotate your books with bookmarks, highlighting, and notes.

Set Up iBooks

Start your iBook experience by setting it up the way you want:

1. Press **Home** and tap **Settings | iBooks** to open the iBooks settings.

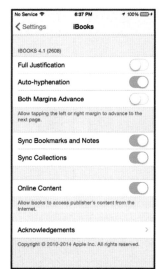

2. Review the settings and consider if you want to change any of them:

   - **Full Justification**, when enabled, aligns the text to the margins on both the left and right edges by spreading out the characters and words. The alternative is to have a ragged right edge with consistent character and word spacing.

   - **Auto-hyphenation**, when enabled, allows splitting words on the right margin to facilitate justification without drastic changes to the character and word spacing.

   - **Both Margins Advance**, when enabled, allows you to advance to the next page on the right by tapping the left margin as well as the right margin. Otherwise, tapping the left margin will take you back one page.

   - **Sync Bookmarks And Notes** and **Sync Collections**, when enabled, sync your bookmarks, notes, and current page information, as well as the way you have organized your books into collections across your iOS devices such as iPads and iPods.

   - **Online Content**, when enabled, allows the book you are reading to go online and access content from the book's publisher.

   - **Acknowledgements** is simply Apple acknowledging the people who contributed to iBooks.

3. Press **Home** to leave Settings.

Search and Buy from the iBookstore

The iBookstore is like the iTunes Store, except that it is for books. Here is how to buy or acquire (some are free) one or more books:

1. From the Home screen, tap **iBooks** and tap **Featured** in the bottom-left area. The iBookstore will open.

2. Swipe from right to left the various lines of books. Swipe up to review various categories of books. You might want to explore Categories at the top left or Top Charts at the bottom center. You can also tap Search and enter to search for specific books, authors, or categories.

3. When you find a book you are interested in, tap it to open detailed information about it.

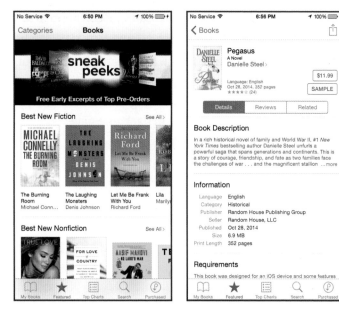

4. If you want to read a sample of the book, tap **Sample**. The book will appear on your bookshelf with the word "Sample" on the cover. Some samples are quite extensive.

5. When you are ready to buy a book, tap the book's price and then **Buy Book**, enter your Apple ID password, and tap **Return**. The book will appear in iBooks.

Use iBooks

Although the principal purpose of iBooks is to facilitate the reading of books, it also provides for the acquiring, organization, display, and disposal of books. The functions that can be performed in iBooks include the following:

- **View books** either in the standard bookshelf view, shown next at left, or in a list view, shown next at right by tapping the stack of lines icon in the upper-left corner.

- **Sort list view** by tapping one of the four sort methods at the top of the list view screen.

- **Arrange books** on the bookshelf by touching and holding on a book while dragging it to another location.

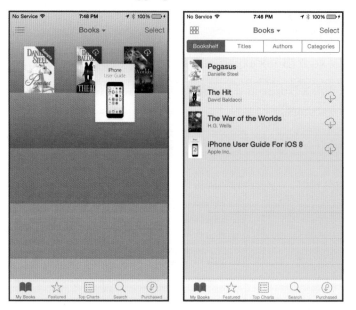

- **Search for a book** by scrolling to the top (swiping from top to bottom) of the bookshelf or book list; tapping in the search box; entering the keywords such as author, title, or subject; and tapping **Search**.

- **Delete a book** in either view by tapping **Select** in the far-upper-right corner and tapping the book (or books) you want to delete to place a white check mark in a blue circle on the book(s). When you are ready, tap **Delete**. You then can tap either **Delete This Copy** to delete the copy on your iPhone or **Delete From All Devices** to delete copies from your iPhone as well as any copies on your other iOS devices. Tap **Done**. The book will remain available to you in iCloud (see the icon in the upper-right corner of the book). Tap the book to bring a copy back onto the iPhone.

- **Organize books** by putting your library into  collections or categories that you set up similar to the categories in list view, but with your own categories (or "collections") that appear in both Bookshelf and list view. Do this by tapping **Select**, selecting the books, tapping **Move**, and selecting the collection or creating a new one.

Read a Book

Using iBook to read a book is quite easy, but iBook also provides the means to do much more than just read—in terms of enlarging the page, changing the font size, jumping to a particular page, jumping to the table of contents, looking up the definition of a word, and adding a bookmark. Not all books that you read in iBooks have exactly the same features, but many have the ones described here:

- From iBook, **swipe the bookshelf** (if needed) to open the collection and then tap the book that you want to read. The book will open. If you have never read any of the book on the iPhone before, it will open to page 1. If you have previously read some of the book on the iPhone or other iOS device with which you are sharing the book, the book will open to where you were last reading.

- **Turn a page** by tapping in the left margin or swiping from the left edge to go back a page, or by tapping in the right margin or swiping from the right edge to go forward a page.

- **Display the controls** by tapping virtually anywhere on the page (although Apple recommends toward the center of the page).

- **Return to the library** by tapping the **Library** button in the upper-left corner.

- **Display the table of contents** or a list of bookmarks or your notes by tapping the **Contents** icon and then tapping either **Bookmarks** or **Notes** (the Contents page is displayed by default).

- **Change the font and size** by tapping the **Fonts** icon to open the Fonts menu, where you can change the brightness using the slider at the top, decrease or increase the font size by repeatedly tapping the smaller or larger "A," change the font by tapping **Fonts** and selecting a font.

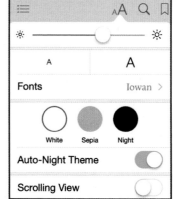

- **Search the text** by tapping the **Search** icon to open the Search box. Type a word or page number to search for and tap **Search**.

- **Add a bookmark** by tapping the **Bookmark** icon on the far right. Tap the icon again to delete it. Because iBook keeps track of where you are currently reading, bookmarks are for other purposes you might have. See a list of bookmarks by tapping the **Contents** icon and then **Bookmarks**.

- **Go to another page** by dragging the slider at the bottom of the page in either direction.

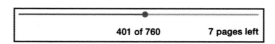

Annotate a Book

For those who like to annotate the books they read, reading in iBook has to be a real asset. Besides leaving bookmarks, as discussed earlier, you can also perform the following tasks:

- **Select text**, any amount of it, by double-tapping some of what you want to select and then dragging the endpoints to enclose all of the text you want to select. When you do that, a menu appears that allows you to copy, get a definition, highlight, make a note, search, or share the selection.

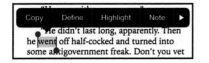

- **Highlight text** by dragging across it or by selecting it and tapping **Highlight**. In the latter case, in the Highlight menu that opens, tap the color discs on the left and then tap one of the five colors or the underline. Close the highlight menu by tapping anywhere outside of the highlight.

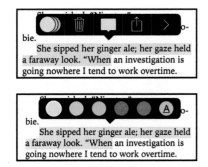

- **Add a note** by selecting the text to be noted and tapping **Note** in the selection menu. A blank note will appear, where you can type the note you want. When you are finished, tap outside the note or highlight. The note will disappear, and a little yellow icon will appear in the margin.

- **Remove highlight and a note** by tapping the highlighted text, tapping **Highlight,** and tapping the recycle bin. If you have a note, you will be told that the note will also be deleted, and you can tap **Cancel** or **Delete**; otherwise, just the highlight will be removed from the text and you are returned to the normal page.

- **Search** by selecting a word and tapping **Search**. A search panel opens displaying the locations in the book where the word appears and allowing you to search the Web and Wikipedia.

TIP Many public libraries, even smaller ones, have programs for lending ebooks on the Internet. You need a library card and a library app such as 3M (used with smaller libraries), OverDrive (which is able to handle multiple library cards), and others. You may be able to choose to get books in different formats. If you choose the Kindle version, it goes through the Amazon store and your device must be registered to your Amazon account. There are differences among libraries on how the ebook lending works, so you'll need to explore your own local library.

Use Maps

iPhone's Maps is one of its most useful and practical apps, as well as being fascinating and even fun. You can quickly find where an address is located as well as get directions to it. You can also see where you are currently and get information about that area, as well as find out about points of interest and local establishments. You can see this in a standard map view, in a 3-D view, in a satellite view, or in a hybrid view, where the street names, points of interest, and establishments are overlaid on the satellite view. If that isn't enough, you can view the satellite and hybrid views straight up and down (so you can better see the streets) or at an angle (so you can better see the buildings). Maps has two primary purposes: to find out where something is located and to get directions to a location.

NOTE Maps requires an Internet connection, either Wi-Fi or cellular, and voice-driving directions require a cellular connection that will incur data usage. To get your current location you must give permission for that. Although maps are relatively accurate and quite useful, they are not perfect and you must allow for some error.

Explore Maps

Maps can be fun to explore, but is also very useful to find out where something is located.

1. From the Home screen, tap **Maps**. Maps will open and show you where you are currently located with a blue dot in a white circle.

2. You can change what you are seeing:
   - Move around a map by dragging it with a single finger.
   - Change the orientation of the map by rotating it with two fingers.
   - Return to the North at the top by tapping the compass in the upper-right corner, which only appears when you have rotated the map.
   - Zoom in by double-tapping with a single finger or by spreading two fingers apart.
   - Zoom out by tapping with two fingers or by bringing together two fingers.

3. Search for a location by tapping in the search box at the top of the screen and typing an address; the name or type of an establishment; or a landmark, area, town, city, ZIP code, or region. Maps may suggest a destination as you are typing. If you want the suggestion, tap it.

4. Touch and hold on a location on the map to drop a pin there, identify it, and mark it for future reference. Tap the info icon in the lower-right corner to change the map view, drop a pin in the center of the map, show a 3-D map, report a problem with the map, or show traffic on local streets using increasingly thicker red dashed lines for increasing traffic congestion and yellow dotted lines for construction.

Standard	Hybrid	Satellite

Drop a Pin

Show 3D Map

Report a Problem

Show Traffic

Data from TOMTOM others ▸

5. Tap one of the many icons on the map to get information about that location or establishment.

6. Tap the arrowhead in the lower-left corner to see your current location.

7. Select **Satellite** and **Show 3D Map** on the Info menu to see an awesome view of buildings in that area.

8. Tap the **Share menu** icon in the upper-right corner to send map information of either your current location or a selected location to others using AirDrop, Message, Mail, or other means.

9. Press the **Home** button and tap **Settings | Maps**. Here, you can control the volume of voice navigation, choose whether distance is in miles or kilometers, and whether labels are in English.

●●●●● Verizon 🗢   11:38 PM   ◀ ✲ 100% ▭ ✦

‹ Settings   **Maps**

NAVIGATION VOICE VOLUME

No Voice

Low Volume

Normal Volume   ✓

Loud Volume

DISTANCES

In Miles   ✓

In Kilometers

MAP LABELS

Always in English   ⬤▭

▷▷ Get Directions

It is one thing to locate a place or an establishment, but it might still be difficult to get there. Maps can show you how to get to a destination with alternative routes on a map, with a set of written instructions, and can give you turn-by-turn voice instructions.

1. From the Maps screen, tap the **Directions** icon in the upper-left corner to open the Directions menu.

   Alternatively, you can open Directions by tapping the automobile symbol on a pin you dropped or that appears when you touch and hold on a map feature or the map itself. You can also tap **Directions To/From Here** in information drop-downs.

2. At the top of the Directions menu, select whether you want directions for driving or walking, or to use third-party apps for directions.

3. Enter or select the starting and ending locations and then tap **Route** to display the route on the map. The recommended route will be shown in dark blue, while alternative routes will be shown in lighter blue with the approximate driving times shown with each route.

4. Start getting voice directions by tapping **Start** at the bottom center. The voice directions will begin and then pause until Maps detects you have completed that step. You can stop the voice directions by tapping **End** in the upper-left corner, change the volume by tapping the loudspeaker in the lower-right corner, or display written directions by tapping **List Steps** in the bottom middle of the screen.

5. Tap **Overview** in the upper-right corner of the voice direction map page to expand the map and see the full route.

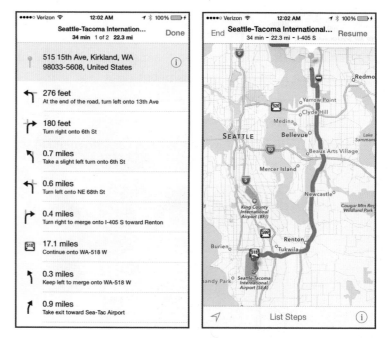

Chapter 8

Exploring Apple Pay and Other Apps

We have covered many of the iPhone's apps in other chapters of this book, but there are still three others that deserve exploring: Passbook with Apple Pay, Health, and Notes. In this chapter we'll look at each and see how they are set up and used.

PAY WITH PASSBOOK

Passbook allows you to store airline boarding passes, movie and concert tickets, coupons, and loyalty cards. It is also where you set up Apple Pay.

▷▷ Set Up Passbook and Apple Pay

Setting up Passbook with an iPhone 6 or 6 Plus is primarily about adding and managing credit cards. Your credit card information is encrypted and kept very securely on your phone—so secure, in fact, that the U.S. government complains they can't get into it! You can set up Passbook and Apple Pay either in the initial Passbook app or in Settings.

Set Up Apple Pay from Passbook

Start by setting up Apple Pay from Passbook.

1. From the iPhone's Home page, tap **Passbook** and in the upper half of the screen tap **Set Up Apple Pay**.

2. Tap **Allow** to allow Passbook and Apple Pay to use your current location for relevant passes, card setup, and store locations.

3. Enter your Apple ID password and tap **OK**. If you have a credit or debit card on file with iTunes and want to use it with Apple Pay, tap that option and go to step 4. Otherwise, tap **Use A Different Credit Or Debit Card** and go to step 5.

4. For your card on file with iTunes, tap in the **Security Code** field and enter the number; then tap **Next | Agree | Agree**. Your card will be activated. When the activation process is complete, you will be told it is ready for Apple Pay. Go to step 6.

5. For a new card, tap in the **Name** field and then correct or enter the name on the card, as needed. Tap in the **Card Number** field and enter the card number (alternatively, tap the camera icon and position the card in the frame; the name, card number, and expiration date will automatically be captured). Finally, tap in the **Security Code** field, enter the number, and then tap **Next | Agree | Agree**. Your card will be activated. When the activation process is complete, you will be told it is ready for Apple Pay.

6. To add more cards (you can store up to eight cards), tap the plus sign in the top-right corner of your list of cards

or tap **Add Another Card** on the initial Passbook screen and return to step 5.

Set Up Passbook and Apple Pay from Settings

Settings provides a similar setup for credit and debit cards, plus allows you to make several other settings.

1. From the iPhone's Home screen, tap **Settings | Passbook & Apple Pay | Add Credit Or Debit Card**.

2. In the Card Details screen that appears, enter your information or use the camera, as described in step 5 under "Set Up Apple Pay from Passbook," earlier in this chapter.

3. Tap **Default Card**, tap the card you want to be your default, and tap **Back**.

4. Tap **Billing Address | Enter New Billing Address**, enter your name and address, and tap **Done**. Alternatively, you can tap **Add From Existing Contact** and select the address you want from your contact list (for example, yourself if you have entered yourself). Unfortunately, the automatic entry in your contacts labeled "Home" is not available to be selected.

5. Tap **Shipping Address | Enter New Shipping Address**, enter your name and address, and tap **Done**.

6. Tap **Email** and enter the necessary information if it is not already there. Do the same thing for **Phone**.

7. To remove a card from your iPhone, tap the card to be removed, scroll down, and tap **Remove Card**.

8. When you are ready, return to the iPhone Home screen.

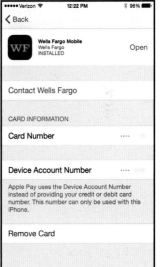

▷▷ Use Apple Pay

With an iPhone 6 or 6 Plus, Apple Pay will allow you to pay for purchases, either while you are online or while you are in a store. This payment is very secure; your credit card information is never seen by the vendor.

Pay at a Store

You can use the iPhone to pay for a purchase in establishments that have contactless reader devices that work with your iPhone. Look for one of the following symbols:

Many stores already (as of fall 2014) support Apple Pay—and the list is growing. A few examples of current stores include Aéropostale, Bloomingdales, Chevron, Macy's, McDonalds, Office Depot, Panera, RadioShack, Staples, Subway, Texaco, and Whole Foods. To use Apple Pay while in one of these establishments, follow these steps:

1. When you are ready to pay, hold your iPhone about an inch away from a contactless reader; there is no need to wake your phone or start an app, and your default credit or debit card will be displayed with "Pay with Touch ID" on the screen).

2. If you want to pay with a different card, tap the default card; your credit and debit cards should appear on the screen.

3. Tap the card you want to use, place your Touch ID finger on the Home button, and continue to hold the iPhone about an inch away from the reader until the iPhone vibrates. If you don't have your finger correctly on the Home button, you will see a message asking you to authenticate with your Touch ID or your passcode. Keep the iPhone in front of the reader until the transaction has been completed, and you will see a check mark and the word "Done." After a moment, the details of the transaction will appear.

Pay Online

Using Apple Pay online simply involves getting the store's Apple Pay app and choosing to use it to pay for a purchase.

1. From the iPhone's Home screen, tap **App Store | Search**, type **Apple Pay**, and tap **Browse Now**. Scroll down to review the list of establishments with apps that allow you to buy online with Apple Pay.

2. Tap **Get | Get | Install | Open** for the establishment where you want to shop. Browse and use the search features to locate what you want to buy. Select it and then tap the Apple Pay logo.

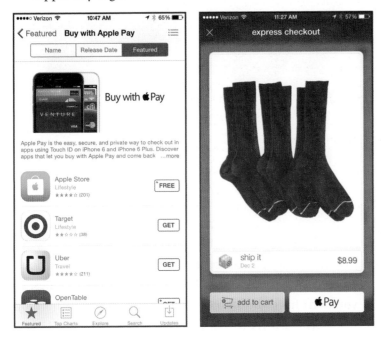

3. In the bill that appears, tap the credit card to select a different one and tap the shipping address and/or contact information to change either one.

4. When you are ready, press the **Home** button with your Touch ID finger to conclude the sale. If you don't want to go ahead, tap **Cancel.**

If you open Passbook, you will see your last transaction and the card it was made with.

》》 Use Passbook

To use Passbook, you need to download or scan in boarding passes, movie and concert tickets, coupons, and gift and reward cards. You can get these in many places, but a good place to start is to download apps that support Passbook. You can open Passbook and tap **Find Apps For Passbook** on the Welcome screen, or you can open itunes.com/passbookapps in Safari or in a browser on your computer.

1. From the iPhone Home screen, tap **Passbook**. If you don't still have the Passbook Welcome screen displayed, tap the plus sign in the upper-right corner to display it.

2. Tap **Find Apps For Passbook** and tap **Get** for several apps that might be useful to you.

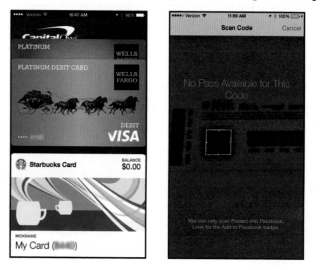

3. Use the app to locate coupons and discount and reward cards. For example, tap **Get | Install | Open With Starbucks**. Tap **Sign Up** and enter your name, email, a password, the month and day of your birthday (for a free coffee), and your postal code. Tap **Continue**, tap **Add Starbucks Card | Get A New Digital Card**, and then tap **Continue** to add the card to Passbook. Identify several Starbucks locations near you, and tap **Add** as the final step to place it in your Passbook. Open Passbook to see the card.

4. You can also scan several types of documents, including retail loyalty and reward cards. Place the document on a flat, nondistracting surface. From the Passbook Welcome screen, tap **Scan Code**, aim the iPhone at the code, and the camera will lock onto it. Unfortunately, not all codes produce a pass.

TRACK YOUR HEALTH

The iPhone's Health app helps you keep track of your fitness and health information so you can track how you are doing in both areas. You can directly enter information, and you can have external devices that use Bluetooth to manually or automatically transfer information to Health.

▶▶ Set Up the Health App

There are three ways to use Health: by directly entering and viewing data (see "Use the Health App," later in this chapter), with separate external devices (follow the instructions for the device), and by using apps that interface with Health, which we'll look at next.

Set Up Health Apps

There are a large number of health- and fitness-related apps, only some of which interface with the iPhone's Health app. Here is how to find and set up the ones that do:

1. From the iPhone's Home screen, tap **App Store | Search**, type **health apps**, and tap **Search**.

2. Under Apps For Health, tap **Browse Now**. In the screen that opens are three categories of apps: Fitness & Wellness, Food & Nutrition, and Healthcare. Drag each category from right to left to see additional apps.

3. Select several apps that are correct for you. Here, I'll get and set up Health Mate, Calorie Counter (by MyFitnessPal), MyChart, and AskMD as examples, not as recommendations (only AskMD interfaces with the Health app).

4. Tap **Health Mate | Get | Install**, sign in to the App Store if necessary, and tap **Open**. If you wish, review their data-gathering devices and then tap **No Devices Yet**.

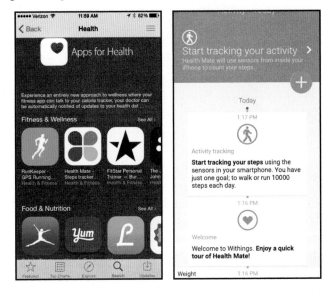

5. Enter the requested information, tap **Next** as needed, and then tap **Create**. Tap the **Welcome** tour and read how to use the app (and get invited to buy their devices). Without their devices, you can still measure your heart rate using your camera, track the number of steps you take if you keep your iPhone in your pocket, and enter your weight and blood pressure that you get from some other devices.

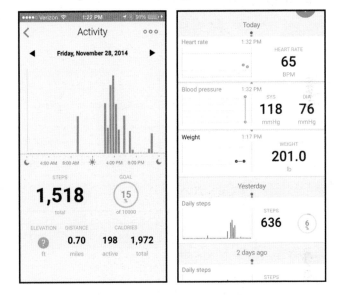

6. From the App Store Apps for Health, tap **Calorie Counter | Get | Install**, sign in to the App Store if necessary, and tap **Open | Sign Up**. Choose to sign up with your email address or your Facebook account and select your weight goal and related information, tapping the right arrow in the upper-right corner as needed.

7. When you have entered all the information, you will be told what your daily calorie goal is. Tap **Start Tracking Now**. Pick a meal, enter a type of food to search for, select a match, and tap **Add (1)**. Repeat for all the items you eat

and for the meals in a day. Tap the day complete icon in the upper-right corner and tap **Complete Entry**. Explore the many aspects of Calorie Counter.

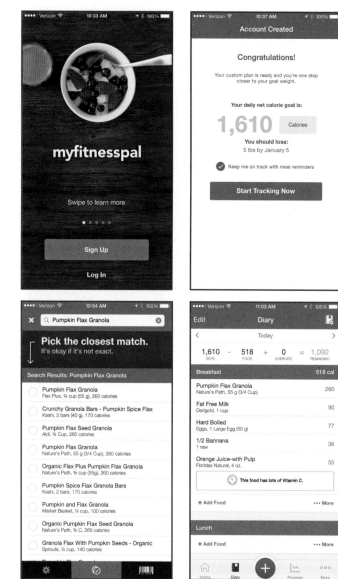

8. From the App Store Apps for Health, tap **MyChart | Get | Install**, sign in to the App Store if necessary, and tap **Open | Accept**. Choose your state and medical provider, sign in, and accept the terms and conditions. This provides some access to the medical records of your medical provider. If your provider is not listed, this app will not work for you.

9. From the App Store Apps for Health, tap **AskMD | Get | Install**, sign in to the App Store if necessary, and tap **Open | Sign Up**. Enter the requested information, tap **Yes** to share information to the Health app, and select the elements you want to share. Browse through the app and use the features that interest you.

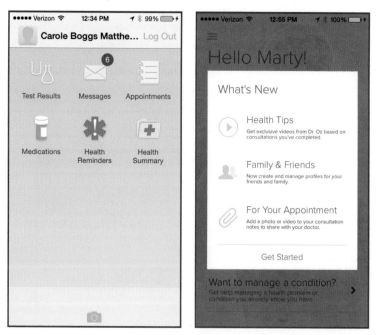

Set Up Emergency Information

The iPhone's Health app provides for the entering of emergency medical information that can be viewed on the lock screen. Here is how to set it up:

1. From the iPhone Home page, tap **Health | Medical ID** in the bottom-right corner and then tap **Create Medical ID**.

2. Choose whether to show this information when the iPhone is locked; then go down through the categories of information and enter what you think is pertinent. Tap **Done** when you are finished. You can always come back and tap **Edit** to make any changes you want.

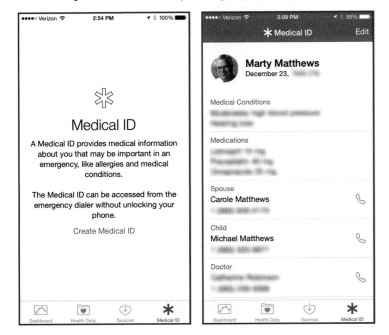

3. To access this information when the phone is locked, press the **Home** button, swipe the screen from left to right, and tap **Emergency | Medical ID**. The information appears.

▷▷ Use the Health App

As stated earlier, the primary use of the Health app is the entering and tracking of fitness and health information. Some of the information can be entered by devices and other apps, and some is generated by the iPhone itself, but much of the information must be entered by you. Once this is entered, Health provides a number of ways to track the information.

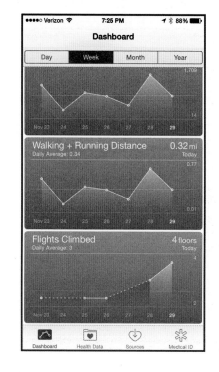

Get Information into Health

Here are some examples of what the iPhone can collect and what you need to enter:

1. From the iPhone Home screen, tap **Health | Health Data** in the bottom left. Here there are seven categories of health and fitness information, plus one that combines all the others.

2. Tap **Body Measurements | Height | Add Data Point**. Enter your height in inches and tap **Add | Back** in the upper-left corner.

3. Tap **Weight | Add Data Point**. Enter your weight in pounds and tap **Add | Back | Health Data** in the upper-left corner.

4. Tap **Fitness | Flights Climbed**. This information is automatically collected by the iPhone, as is Steps and Walking + Running Distance. You can add more data points if you wish. Return to Health Data when you are ready.

5. Tap **Nutrition**. Tap a nutritional element you want to track, tap **Add Data Point**, and enter the amount of that element. Return to Nutrition and repeat this step for other elements. When you are done, return to Health Data.

6. Tap **Sleep | Sleep Analysis | Add Data Point**, enter the start and end dates and times, and tap **Add**. Return to Health Data.

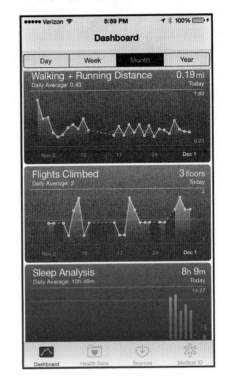

7. Tap **Vitals | Blood Pressure | Add Data Point**, enter the systolic and diastolic figures, and tap **Add**. Return to Vitals.

8. Tap **Heart Rate | Add Data Point**, enter the beats per minute, and tap **Add**. Return to Health Data.

Track Health Information

Once you enter information, you want to see the results and your progress in achieving goals. This is accomplished in two ways: the dashboard, where you can see a selected set of charts, and in the charts for each element. When you enter a particular element, you can see and analyze the chart for that element. Also, you can choose whether you want to show the element on the dashboard by tapping that option.

TAKE NOTES

Notes is very handy, allowing you to record brief ideas, reminders, and lists and to organize those in limited ways. Notes can be shared through iCloud with other Apple devices and through the mail accounts you have. You can also share notes with others and print them.

▷▷ Use Notes

Using Notes is simplicity itself:

1. From the iPhone's Home screen, tap **Notes | New** and begin typing the note. The first line you type will be used as the title of the note.

2. When you are finished, tap **Done | Back** to return to the list of your notes. That's all there is to it. Here are two examples of notes:

3. As you create notes, a list is built on the opening page that allows you to quickly select and return to any note.

TIP You can dictate a note by tapping the microphone key in the onscreen keyboard, dictating the text you want, including punctuation (for example, by saying "period," "colon," or "new paragraph"), and tapping **Done** when you are finished. You may need to do some editing, but dictating should still be faster. Here are screenshots of before and after editing a to do list:

Edit Notes

Notes can be edited like any other text that has been entered into the iPhone.

1. From your list of notes, tap the one you want to edit and then tap anywhere in the note to place the insertion point. You are then asked if you want to select the word or select all of the text.

2. If you tap **Select**, you can drag the selection handles on either end of the selection to select the text you want to work on.

3. When you have the desired selection, you will be asked if you want to cut, copy, replace, or format it. Based on the choice you make, complete the process.

4. Repeat steps 1 through 3, as needed, to complete editing the text. When you are finished, tap **Done | Back**.

5. To delete a note, tap it in the list of notes, tap **Delete** (the trash can) in the lower-left corner, and tap **Delete Note**. Alternatively, in the list of notes, you can swipe a note from right to left and tap **Delete**.

6. To create a new note while you are in a note, tap the **New Note** icon in the lower-right corner.

7. To search notes from the list of notes, drag the top down, tap in the **Search box** that appears, type what you want to search for, tap **Search** in the keyboard, and then tap the appropriate note. The word or phrase you are searching for will be highlighted.

> **NOTE** You cannot sort notes alphabetically, though that would be a great addition. Instead, they show according to the last one opened.

Share and Print Notes

You can share notes with others and print them on a wireless printer.

1. From the list of notes, tap the one you want to share and then tap the **Share** icon in the bottom middle of the screen.

2. In the Share menu that opens, tap the means of sharing you want to use, fill out the sending document, and tap **Send**.

3. To print, tap **Print** in the Share menu, select the number of copies, select the appropriate printer, and tap **Print**.

▷▷ Set Up Notes

You can attach notes to iCloud or to any of your mail accounts that accept notes, such as Gmail and Yahoo! To do that, you must turn on Notes in iCloud and mail accounts and then select the primary account in Notes with these steps:

NOTE You do not need to enable Notes in iCloud and your mail accounts if you do not foresee a need for their use. If you just want to use Notes on your iPhone and don't have other devices or needs for notes, you can ignore the Notes settings discussed here.

1. From the iPhone's Home page, tap **Settings | iCloud | Notes** to allow iCloud to receive and pass on to other Apple devices the notes you create. Tap **Settings** to return there.

2. From Settings, tap **Mail Contacts Calendar** and tap the mail account you want to reflect Notes. For example, tap **Gmail** and tap **Notes** to turn it on if it is currently off. Tap **Mail** in the upper-left corner when you are ready.

3. Repeat step 2 for as many mail accounts as you want to reflect Notes. Tap **Settings** in the upper-left corner when you are ready.

4. From Settings, tap **Notes | Default Account** and tap the account that you want to reflect your notes. If you want them only on your iPhone, tap that choice. Tap **Notes | Settings** in the upper-left corner when you are ready.

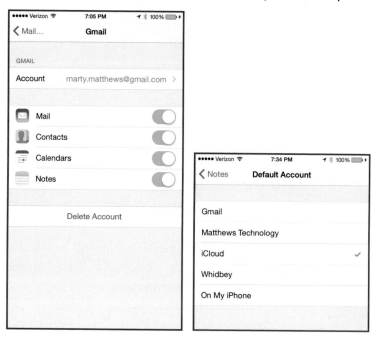

Chapter 9

Socializing and Playing Games

You have seen the iPhone's practical and entertaining sides; in this chapter you'll see its socializing and fun sides: interacting with your family and friends, and playing games. This chapter shows you how to get connected and use Twitter and Facebook, as well as find, download, and use a few of the many games available on the iPhone, some of which are multiplayer games where you can interact with your friends.

FOLLOW TWITTER

Twitter is a social networking service on the Internet that allows you to post very small messages, called "Tweets," of no more than 140 characters. You can choose to follow this stream of messages, or Tweets, on any topic and from any individual. You can also choose to add your own Tweets, which anyone can read. You can read the public postings of anyone else and sign up to follow anyone.

▶▶ Enable and Explore Twitter

You must register with Twitter before you can use it. You can access Twitter from Safari at Twitter.com, or you can download for free the Twitter app from the App Store. The app is tailored to your iPhone, so begin by downloading the app and then registering with Twitter. Next, locate some information and contributors you want to follow. Finally, you can post Tweets of your own and build a following.

Download and Register with Twitter

Use the following steps to download and register with Twitter:

1. From the Home screen, tap the **App Store | Search**. Clear the Search box if needed. Type **twitter** and then tap **Twitter** in the search results.

2. Tap **Free | Install**, use Touch ID or enter your Apple ID password, and tap **OK**. The Twitter app will be downloaded. Tap **Open** to display Twitter. If you want, tap **Allow** to allow Twitter to use your current location.

3. If you don't have an existing Twitter account, tap **Sign Up** and enter the requested information. Otherwise, enter the email address and password for your existing Twitter account. Tap **Don't Allow** or **OK** to allow notifications.

4. You are asked if you want to follow your friends. Tap **OK**, if you wish, to allow access to your contacts. A list of people, including some of your contacts who are on Twitter, will be displayed. Tap the check box on the right for each person you want to follow, or tap **Select All** to do that.

5. Tap **Next** or, if you selected some people, tap **Follow** to display a list of your contacts who are not on Twitter and whom you can invite to join Twitter and follow you. Tap **Invite** to display a list of people who your friends are following and are suggested as people you might want to follow. Tap the check box for each one you want to follow, or tap **Select All** to do that and then tap **Follow**.

6. You are asked if you want to add your photo to your Twitter account, and you are given the option of taking a photo with the iPhone or choosing an existing photo. If you choose the latter, you are asked if you want to allow Twitter access to your photos. Tap **OK** or **Don't Allow** (if you choose Don't Allow, you will need to take a photo and insert it, unless you choose not to have a photo on Twitter). Select the photo you want, move and scale it, and tap **Use | Finish**.

Search for Tweets

In setting up Twitter, you've added the people in your contacts list who you want to follow, but it is likely that you want to follow others in areas that you are interested in. I'm interested in the

Apple Watch and what people are saying about it. Also, I like to cook, so I am interested in new and unique recipes. I can search on both of these topics to see who is Tweeting about them.

1. Tap the **Search** icon, type what you want to search for, and then tap the result you want to explore. In my case, I type and then tap **Apple Watch** to get this screen:

2. Scroll down the Tweets until you see one you might want to follow and then tap it. The selected Tweet will expand.

3. Tap the **Follow** icon if you want to follow this Tweeter or subject.

4. Repeat the first three steps for as many subjects as you want to follow.

TIP Some subjects, such as my interest in cooking, can provide a great many Tweeters to follow, many of whom do a lot of Tweeting.

Explore What Else Is Happening

After you have selected several people and organizations that you want to follow, tap the left arrow in the upper-left corner. This opens the Home page, which displays the Tweets of those you are following.

In addition to the Home page, there are two more pages titled "Discover" and "Activity." The Discover page shows you what is trending, both in general and with those you are following. The Activity page displays the Tweets of people and organizations being followed by those you are following.

1. With the iPhone in portrait orientation and Twitter's Home page displayed, swipe the page from right to left to display the Discover page and swipe again to display the Activity page.

2. On either page, scroll down to see additional Tweets. Tap one of the Tweets to explore it further. It may lead you to a website, and that may lead you to other sites.

3. When you have explored a path as far as you want, return to Twitter by tapping the **X** in the upper-left corner.

4. Beneath each of the Tweets on the Home, Discover, and Activity pages is a set of four icons (three on the Home page

and one for Tweets from those you are already following), as shown here:

- **Reply** Used to send a Tweet to the person or organization that posted the Tweet you are replying to.
- **Retweet** Used to repost the Tweet under your name; tap **Retweet** a second time to undo it.
- **Favorite** Used to state that the Tweet is one of your favorites.
- **Follow** Used to add the Tweeter to those you follow.

Post Tweets and Build a Following

Although reading the Tweets of others can be interesting and worthwhile, there is an equally compelling use of Twitter: to state your thoughts and comments by posting your own Tweets, with and without photos, by replying to the Tweets of others, and by retweeting what others have posted.

Post a Tweet

Posting Tweets is no harder than posting a text message, except that you are limited to 140 characters, and, of course, you must figure out what to say in that number of characters. Here are the steps to follow:

1. On any Twitter page, tap the **Tweet** icon in the upper-right corner to open the new Tweet message area.

2. Type whatever you want to say in the message area. Notice the number in the upper right, which starts at 140 and decreases as you type, telling you the number of characters you have left.

3. When you are ready, tap **Tweet** in the upper-right corner to post on Twitter.

4. If you are not already there, tap the Twitter Home screen ("Timelines" in the bottom-left corner) and you will see what you posted.

Tweet with Photos and Add Your Location

You may have noticed two icons in the lower-left corner of the New Tweet dialog box. These allow you to add a photo to your Tweet and to add your location. Here's how:

1. Create and enter a new Tweet, as described previously.

2. Tap the **Photo** icon in the lower-right corner.

3. Tap the **Location** icon to be asked if you want to add your current location to your Tweets. Tap **Enable** to do that, or tap **Cancel** to not add your location.

4. When the Tweet is ready, tap **Tweet** to send it.

Tailor Twitter Settings

You can change Twitter settings in both the iPhone's settings and in Twitter.

1. From the iPhone's Home screen, tap **Settings | Twitter**. Tap your account to change your password and/or description. Tap **Find Me By Email** to allow people to search Twitter and find you using your email address.

2. Also in iPhone Settings you can add another Twitter account, either existing or new. You can also update your possible Twitter followings based on changes to your contacts as well as allow Twitter to use your Apple account so that you sign in to Twitter when you sign in to your iPhone.

3. While in iPhone Settings, tap **Notifications | Twitter** and choose the notification settings for Tweets that are correct for you. Return to the iPhone Home screen when you are finished.

4. Tap **Twitter | Me** and tap **Edit Profile** in the upper right to change your photo, header image, name, location, website, and bio. Tap **Save** when you are ready.

5. Tap the **gear icon** and then **Settings** to change your account, image upload quality, sound effects, image previews, notifications timeline, text size, and accessibility. Tap **Done** when you are ready.

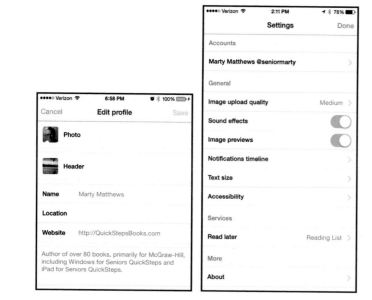

EXPLORE FACEBOOK

Facebook allows people 13 and older to connect with their friends and share comments, pictures, and videos. To do that, each user, after registering, creates their own web page and identifies the friends they want to share with. You can limit sharing to just your friends, or have a public page that anyone can view. You can send invitations to people to be your Facebook friends, and you will likely receive invitations from others to be their friends. Making full use of Facebook is a book-length subject, and my wife, Carole Matthews, has written one—*Facebook for Seniors QuickSteps*—published by McGraw-Hill Education.

Start Using Facebook

As with Twitter, you can use Facebook either through Safari or with the app, which you can download for free from the App Store. Also, as with Twitter, I recommend using the app. Once you get Facebook open, even if it is for the first time, you can immediately start using it by posting comments, photos, and videos. You will want to add friends who can see and respond to what you have posted.

Download and Register with Facebook

Use the following steps to download and register with Facebook:

1. From the Home screen, tap the **App Store**. Clear the Search box, type **facebook**, and then tap **Facebook** in the search results.

2. Tap **Free | Install**, enter your Apple ID password, and tap **OK**. The Facebook app will be downloaded. Tap **Open** to display Facebook.

3. If you don't have an existing Facebook account, tap **Sign Up For Facebook** and enter the requested information, choose a picture of you to use (you have to give Facebook permission to use your photos), and tap **Get Started**. Choose to find friends by allowing Facebook to use your contacts list. Finally, confirm your email address to Facebook. Otherwise, enter the email address and password for your existing Facebook account. Facebook will open.

Use Facebook

If you have an existing Facebook account, your current Facebook page will open; otherwise, you are asked where you want to start.

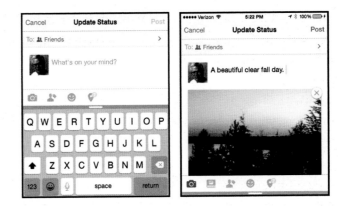

1. Tap **Status** in the upper-left corner. Select whether you want your status to go to just your friends, everybody ("public"), or just selected friends, and then enter what's on your mind or comment that you would like to share with others. When you have completed entering the comment, tap **Post**. Your status or comment will appear on your page.

2. Tap the **Photo** icon in the lower-left corner to add one. Tap either the **Camera** icon in the upper-left corner and take a photo as you normally would, or choose from the Camera Roll a photo you want, and then tap **Post**.

3. Tap **Check In** in the upper-right corner. Facebook will ask if it can turn on Location Services. If that is acceptable to you, from the iPhone's Home screen, tap **Settings | Facebook | Settings | Location | While Using The App**. If you allow the use of your current location, Facebook will display a list of Facebook pages that are close to you.

4. Tap the **Message** icon (the silhouette and three bars) in the upper-left corner to open the list of your friends to whom you can send individual messages. To send a message, tap the friend's name, tap in the text box at the bottom of the screen, type a message, and tap **Send**.

Add and Contact Friends

At the bottom of the Facebook screen are five icons for five areas of Facebook. The Facebook discussion so far has dealt with the default News Feed area. This is where posts that you receive are displayed. The second area is Requests, which shows you the friend requests you have received, people you may know (generally friends of friends) and whom you may request to be your Facebook friend, and allows you to expand the people you may know and search for others.

You need to start out with a few friends on Facebook. With that start, the number of your friends will quickly grow as you get suggestions to add friends of friends. Also, others will request that you be their friend as they learn you are on Facebook.

1. Tap **Requests** at the bottom of the Facebook screen and review the friend requests at the top of the screen. Tap **Confirm** for those you want to be your friend, and tap **Delete** for others.

2. For all the people on the Friend Requests page, tap the person's photograph to open the person's Facebook page. From an individual's page you may tap pictures to enlarge them, tap **View Profile** at the bottom center to see more about the person, and swipe from right to left to see other friend requests.

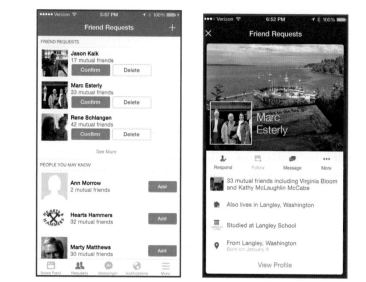

3. From the summary Friends Request page, tap the plus sign in the upper-right corner to open the Find Friends page. Here, you can see several ways to add friends. If you are just starting out, you will probably not see any people under Suggestions or Requests.

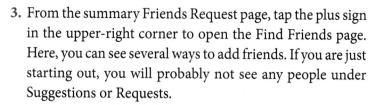
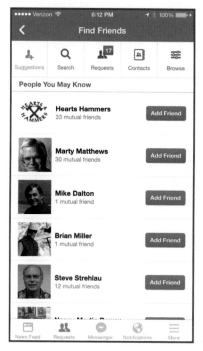

4. Tap **Search | Name Or Email** and type a friend's name or email address (an email address is preferred because if you enter a name, you must search through all the people on Facebook with the same name—which is probably a lot). Finally, tap **Search**.

5. When you see a friend you would like to add, tap that friend's name to open their page and then tap **Add Friend**. You will see the label "Add Friend" change to "Undo." Under the name you will see "Request Sent."

6. If needed, tap the return arrow in the upper-left corner to return to the Find Friends page and then tap **Contacts** to see who on your contacts page is on Facebook. Tap **Get Started** and then **OK** to proceed. A list of people from your address book and on Facebook will appear. Tap **Add Friend** opposite the people you want to be your friends. They will receive a notice like this:

7. You can then tap **Skip** and look at everybody else in your address book. Tap **Invite** to invite them to create a Facebook page and be your friend. Tap **Done** when you are ready.

8. Tap **Browse** to search for people from organizations and institutions you are affiliated with.

9. After adding several requests for friends, tap **Suggestions**. You will see that you now have a number of suggestions based on the requests you have made and who their friends are. Tap the **Add Friend** icon on the right of the people you want to be your friends.

10. After your friends have had a chance to see their email and respond, you will see them in the right column on your News Feed page. If you tap the **Notification** icon in the

bottom of the page, you will see the friends who accepted your requests.

NOTE When you start using Facebook, be prepared to receive a lot of suggestions and requests for friends.

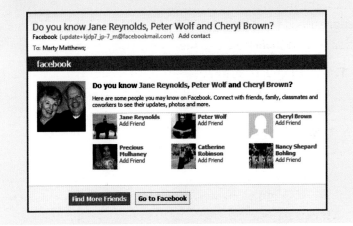

⏩ Manage Your Facebook Account

Facebook can disseminate a lot of information about you, and it is important that you use the controls that Facebook provides to place the limitations you want on who can see what. There are two lists of settings you can work with to have Facebook behave the way you want: the iPhone's settings and Facebook's settings.

Review iPhone's Facebook Settings

The iPhone's Facebook settings have to do with whether apps can use your Facebook account and whether Facebook can use other iPhone apps.

1. On the iPhone Home page, tap **Settings | Facebook | Settings**. Review the apps that Facebook can access. The default is all those listed. Tap any you don't want accessed.

Adjust Facebook's Own Settings

Facebook has several different places where there are settings, and they duplicate each other in some cases. Here, I'll try to point out some of the more important ones, but it is worthwhile for you to review them. There are far more than can be listed here.

1. In Facebook, tap **More** (the three bars in the lower-right corner).

2. Drag or scroll the list of options up until you see the primary heading Settings and tap **Privacy Shortcuts** to open what is probably the most important of Facebook Settings.

2. Tap **Facebook** in the top-left corner and tap your name. Here, you can enter your password and delete your Facebook account from your iPhone (it does not delete your Facebook account).

3. In the list of apps that can use your Facebook account, which are all selected by default, select the ones you do not want to use it.

4. If you want Facebook to have temporary access to the email addresses and phone numbers of your contacts, tap **Update All Contacts**.

3. Tap **Who Can See My Stuff | Who Can See My Future Posts**, choose the category of friends to do this, and tap the return arrow in the upper-left corner.

4. Tap **Where Do I Review…**, review your Activity Log and see who saw the items you posted and liked, and tap the return arrow in the upper-left corner.

5. Tap **Who Can Contact Me** and then under **Whose Messages Do I Want Filtered**, choose the level of filtering you want.

6. Tap **Who Can Send Me Friend Requests**, choose the option you want, and tap the return arrow in the upper-left corner.

7. Tap **How Do I Stop Someone…**, enter the name of the person to be stopped, and tap the return arrow in the upper-left corner to return to the overall Facebook settings page.

8. Scroll down and tap **Settings** under the Settings heading. Tap each of the 13 categories, review the options, make the changes that are correct for you, and tap the return arrow in the upper-left corner.

CAUTION! Consider carefully the information you put on Facebook and the degree to which you allow others to view your information. Even though you put limits on who can see your information, a good assumption is that anything you put on Facebook is public information. In your exploring Facebook, use common sense to protect yourself, as discussed in the "Protecting Your Online Identity" QuickFacts.

QuickFacts

Protecting Your Online Identity

It is a wonderful thing to be able to find and exchange information with people with similar interests. Social networking facilitates these communications so that we connect with broader webs of people, as well as with people we simply do not know. In today's world, though, it is wise to be "street smart" when it comes to the streets of the Internet. Here are a few hard-and-fast rules for keeping your identity to yourself and your information private:

- Make sure your password is reasonably difficult to figure out and protect your passwords by not sharing them and by changing them often.

- Be wise about the information you put on the Internet and by not putting on highly personal information.

- Don't click links from unknown persons or organizations. These can be programmed to gather information from you or your computer. Check the actual URL of people soliciting your information and make sure they are who you think they are.

Social networking can be fun and a great way to meet people and interact with them. Just keep in mind that you want to be "street smart" while you are having that great time.

By looking at only Twitter and Facebook, I have only touched on social networking apps—although they are far and away the most popular ones, especially for seniors. If you are interested in business and job networking, I recommend looking at LinkedIn, and if you want to share a common interest, I recommend Pinterest as an iPhone app. Talk to your friends and associates about what they are using and possibly try out other social networking apps.

PLAY GAMES

Almost everybody likes to play games. The iPhone App Store offers a large number of them you can directly play, and the iPhone's Game Center allows you to compete with others in multiplayer games and to keep track of how you are doing. The Game Center is separate from individual games themselves, so we'll discuss them first.

▷▷ Download and Play Games

Many iPhone games are free, or at least start out free, and many more cost something (from 99 cents on up). Just to find a game you want is a major undertaking, and to make sure it is well thought of and fun to play takes research. There are many different types of games, such as action games, board games, card games, and many others. You can limit yourself to free games, knowing that many "free" games get you hooked during free play and then have various ways to get you to pay something. Although we'll discuss several games here, I suggest that you do some initial research by typing **best iPhone games** or **best free iPhone games** into Google or Bing and reading through the reviews. If you are looking for a particular type of game, enter **best card games on iPhone**, for example.

Back on your iPhone, open the App Store and perform searches on games in general, free games, and then on particular types of games. In what follows I'll describe two games I think are fun to play and well crafted as examples of the many types available.

Solitaire

The card game Solitaire has been on the iPhone since the beginning. If you perform an iPhone App Store search on Solitaire, you will see a number of games. One that I like is the free version by Finger Arts. It does have ads, but they appear at the bottom of the screen.

You can choose the look of the cards by tapping that option at the lower left and make other settings by tapping **Options** on the right. You can also jump right in and begin playing by clicking **Play** and then choosing a difficulty and the number of cards to draw. At that point, you can tap the card deck on the upper right to begin play.

Mahjong

Mahjong is an ancient Chinese game where you try to use up all the tiles by matching them. You tap first one tile and then a matching tile and the two disappear, allowing you to see and work with other tiles. The 1001 Ultimate Mahjong version of this game is free, but has some in-app purchases you can make. The free version of the game without additions plays well.

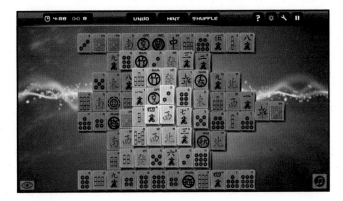

When the game first opens, you are asked to choose from many different initial layouts of the tiles. You also can tap **Options** and choose from a number of tile sets, backgrounds, and themes, as well as set the volume. Upon choosing a layout, the game is created. Work from the top down and the edges in. It is truly addictive.

▷▷ Explore the Game Center

The Game Center is not where you go to play games. You play games by starting them from the Home screen. Game Center is where you keep track of how well you are doing and, most importantly, where you connect with others who play the same games as you and challenge them to play against you. The Game Center helps you connect with other players, keeps track of the accomplishments of you and your opponents, and tells you about other multiplayer games.

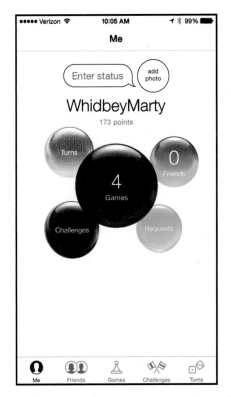

events. *See also* Calendar (*cont.*)
  deleting, 79
  editing, 79
  information about, 78
  inviting people to, 78, 81–82
  listing in Calendar, 74
  time zones, 77–78
  URLs for, 78, 79
Exchange accounts, 33, 56

F

face detection, 94
Facebook, 156–162
  adding/contacting friends, 157–159
  apps accessed by, 159
  calendar, 81
  Contacts groups, 33
  downloading/registering, 156
  managing account, 159–162
  overview, 156
  password, 160, 161
  precautions, 161
  privacy, 160–161
  settings, 159–161
  updating contacts, 160
  using, 157
Facebook app, 156
FaceTime, 112–113
  cellular service and, 112
  described, 20
  Do Not Disturb option, 21, 89–90
  ending calls, 113
  initiating calls, 112–113
  muting audio, 28, 113
  resolution and, 2, 96
  resuming, 113
  switching camera orientation, 113
  turning calls into FaceTime calls, 28
  turning on/off, 9
FaceTime app, 2

FaceTime button, 28
FaceTime camera, 2, 3, 93
Favorites list
  calling from, 29
  deleting entries, 29
  managing, 29
  working with entries, 29
Favorites setting, 41
files
  audio/video, 48
  email attachments, 63–66
  memory used by, 4, 109
  sharing. *See* sharing
  size, 109
  viewing, 98
filters (camera effects), 96, 97, 105
Find My iPhone, 7, 9
finger movements, 18–19, 22
fingerprint identity sensor, 3, 9–10, 140
flash, camera, 2, 95, 96
Flash technology, 48
flash, True Tone, 2, 3
flashlight, 2, 91, 96
flicking, 18, 22
folders
  bookmarks, 46–47
  email, 66–68, 69
  music, 118
  photos, 64, 102, 103
forms. *See* web forms
forwarding calls, 32
Fraudulent Website Warning, 42, 50–51

G

game apps, 162
Game Center, 20, 162, 163
games, 162–163
  downloading, 162
  free, 162, 163
  Mahjong, 163

  playing, 162–163
  searching for, 162
  Solitaire, 162
  types of, 162
GB (gigabyte), 5
General Packet Radio Service (GPRS) service, 21
Genius playlists, 125
gigabyte (GB), 5
Gmail, 56, 57, 58, 68
Google search engine, 44
GPRS (General Packet Radio Service) service, 21
GPS, 7
group messaging, 71

H

HD (high-definition) video, 108, 110
HDR (High Dynamic Range), 96
HDR photo series, 97
HDR photos, 108
headphone jack, 2, 3, 4. *See also* EarPods
headphones, 4, 125
Health app, 142–147
  adding medical information, 146–147
  AskMD app, 143, 144
  blood pressure, 147
  described, 20
  emergency information, 145
  health/fitness-related apps, 143–144
  heart rate, 147
  Medical ID, 145
  medical records, 144
  nutrition information, 146
  setting up, 142–145
  sleep information, 147
  tracking health information, 147
  using, 145–147
  vitals, 147
Health Mate app, 143
health/fitness-related apps, 143–144
"Hey Siri" option, 27

R

radio. *See* iTunes Radio
Reader mode (Safari), 48, 128
reading, 127–136
  with iBooks. *See* iBooks
  with Newsstand, 128–129
  public library ebooks, 133
  with Safari, 127–128
Reading List, 39, 40, 42
Recents list, 29
red handset button, 28
redo options, 26
release hold, 3
Reload icon, 39
reloading websites, 39
Reminders, 19, 84–85. *See also* alerts
resolution, 2, 96
RETURN key, 12
ringer, 2, 3
ringer volume, 2, 3
ring/silent switch, 2, 3
ringtones, 2, 36
ripping CDs, 118, 120

S

Safari, 38–52. *See also* web browsers
  autofill settings, 41, 42
  blocking pop-ups, 41–42
  bookmarks, 45–47
  browsing Internet, 42–44, 53
  clearing cache, 42
  clearing history, 42
  controls, 39–41
  cookies, 42, 49–50
  described, 20
  Do Not Track option, 42, 50
  Fraudulent Website Warning, 42, 50–51
  introduction to, 38–42

  navigation, 39, 43–44, 47, 48
  Open Links settings, 41
  opening websites in, 39, 42–43
  passwords, 41
  Private Browsing option, 50
  Reader mode, 48, 128
  Reading List, 39, 40, 42
  reading with, 127–128
  search engine choice, 41
  searching, 41, 44, 51–52
  settings, 41–42
  Web Inspector, 42
screen, 17–23. *See also* Home screen
  brightness, 90
  described, 4
  finger movements, 18–19
  illustrated, 3
  image/text size on, 10
  lock rotation, 90
  locking, 21
  overview, 17
  rotation, 21
screen captures, 101
Screen rotation locked, 21
screenshots, 101
scrolling, 18
Search Engine settings, 41
search engines, 39, 41, 44
searching
  Calendar, 75
  email messages, 69–70
  Favorites, 41
  iBookstore, 129–130
  Internet, 44, 51–52
  iTunes, 117–118
  iTunes Store, 117–118
  within open web page, 49
  Preload Top Hit, 41
  Quick Website Search, 41
  from Safari, 44

  with Spotlight, 23
  Spotlight Suggestions, 41
  for text in books, 132, 133
  via search engines, 39, 41, 44
security. *See also* passcode; passwords
  cookies, 42, 49–50
  Do Not Track option, 42, 50
  Fraudulent Website Warning, 42, 50–51
  Internet, 49–51
  Location Services and, 7–8, 21
  phishing, 42
  privacy. *See* privacy
  Private Browsing option, 50
security questions, 9
selecting text, 25–26
"selfies," 96
self-timer, camera, 96
Settings app, 20
Shake to Shuffle, 125
Share icon, 64
Share menu, 39, 48
Shared Links, 39, 40
Shared Streams, 101
sharing
  AirDrop, 39, 83, 90, 91
  calendars, 82–84
  Home Sharing, 125
  notes, 149
  photos, 101, 103, 106–107, 108
  video, 112
  website address, 39–40
SHIFT key, 12
shopping on Internet, 52–53
Short Message Service (SMS), 71
sidebar, 13
silent/ring switch, 2
SIM card, 3
SIM card release hold, 3
SIM card tray, 3

Wi-Fi service, 5
Wikipedia, 51
Windows computers. *See also* computer
  connecting iPhone to, 5, 12–13
  system requirements, 5

wireless networks. *See* Wi-Fi networks
word definitions, 26
World Clock, 86
World Wide Web, 38–47. *See also* Internet

Y

Yahoo! email accounts, 56
Yahoo! search engine, 44
YouTube, 112